GRAVITAS

GRAVITAS

DR LOUISE MAHLER

WILEY

First published in 2024 by John Wiley & Sons Australia, Ltd
Level 4, 600 Bourke St, Melbourne, Victoria 3000, Australia

Typeset in Plantin Std Regular 11.5pt/15.5pt

© John Wiley & Sons Australia, Ltd 2024

The moral rights of the author have been asserted

ISBN: 978-1-394-23733-3

A catalogue record for this
book is available from the
National Library of Australia

Disclaimer

CONTENTS

CONTENTS

ACKNOWLEDGEMENTS

My long-deceased mother was obsessed with ancient Greece and ancient Rome. In fact, she was so interested that in her sixties, she went back and did a degree in ancient history, travelled extensively in Greece and Rome, and collected an astounding library. Meanwhile, back at the ranch, I turned a blind eye.

Isn't that life? Sometimes it is right in front of you and you miss it (which is the point of this book!). So I'd like to take this opportunity to rectify the situation and say thank you to my mother for sharing the enthusiasm that eventually penetrated every bone in my body with fascination when the context of that work related to the area of gravitas (as opposed to my mother's passion for the visual). So, firstly I acknowledge my mother for her passion and perseverance.

Next, during my time singing, I came in contact with people who were incredibly important to me, with whom I worked and who helped mould my thinking about discipline, humour, the importance of the body and the art of singing, including Dame Elisabeth Schwarzkopf, Sir Peter Pears, Sir Peter Ustinov and Professor Ellen Müller-Preis. All are now gone, but none are forgotten.

More recently there is a team of people around me to thank profusely who inspire and support on a daily basis.

First is my incredible colleague and friend Jane Anderson, who I admire tremendously and is a constant source of inspiration and support. Then there is Meldrick Advincula, whose aim—to be the best assistant in the world—is a goal he may have just achieved (and no, you cannot have him).

Thank you also to Emily Baxter for keeping the social media fire burning and Randal Killip for helping me get the message out to the broadcast media. I couldn't have done this without any of you.

The impetus for this book was born from a chance purchase many years ago of a wonderful book by Gregory Aldrete (*Gestures and Acclamations in Ancient Rome*) that captured my attention and sparked a fascination. This was the spark that began my journey to translate my ideas, break the modern-day paradigms that are holding us back from communicating with gravitas and produce something I hope will be useful to others.

Thank you to Kristen Lowrey, whose thoughtful editing and inputs helped me make sense of work that is not necessarily suited to the printed form. And thank you to the team at Wiley, with special mention to Lucy Raymond for having faith in me right from the start.

Across Australia, there are many friends who have helped to keep up my spirits (you know who you are), while my Yarra Valley family—Karen Maynard, Dale May, Maddison Horsley and Jack Horsley—have kept the home fires burning and been constant, faithful companions for whom love has no boundaries.

With my wonderful two children Oliver and Colette being fabulous and conquering the world in different parts of the globe, I thank you both for your support. And it would be remiss to leave out the ever-present passion of my life—Kangaroo Manor. If you can love a property, I love mine because it is alive with inspiration.

Apart from the 300 kangaroos, five koalas and many wombats I adore, Kangaroo Manor is also home to Gilbert and Sullivan, the happiest Golden Retrievers in the world; Charlie and Boots, two ridiculous donkeys; and Sir James and Two Stroke, my decades-long equine companions. Yes, they are horses, but they are friends and teachers too, and maybe being with them takes me to a time of warriorship in ancient Rome.

I'd also like to thank my clients, who play a major role in my life. You have been willing chess pieces in the game of piecing all this together, and I thank you for your trust and respect (the keys to gravitas).

I thank you all for allowing me to be creative, discover things others have forgotten and imagine things in our modern world—the things we must never forget.

PREFACE

How Opera Taught Me the Key to Gravitas

Would it surprise you to learn that the first nugget of an idea for this book came from opera—more specifically, from my life performing in the world of opera? But then I have come to believe that life is an opera or a *fabula praetexta* (an ancient Roman drama with a theme or legend from Roman history), and so I should not be surprised that opera is precisely where this idea started.

My career in singing was not about talent, but regime. Like an Olympian training, as singers we kept fit, we practised at length, we never sang popular music and we had few friends, if any, outside the world of classical music. Life was insular but tremendously fulfilling in the simple rewards of doing what we did well and being praised for it. It was a total discipline.

As a performer, I sang, studied, lived and made friends with some distinguished figures in the opera world, including those famed in the industry such as Sir Peter Ustinov and Dame Elisabeth Schwarzkopf, and was fortunate to be consumed by their worlds of excellence.

As Rodelinda in *Rodelinda* at the Aldeburgh Festival

In Europe, we sang and communicated in at least five different languages, relying heavily on the use of signing to help our audience understand despite the language barriers. Whatever the language we were singing in, when we appeared on stage we worked to engage our audience at an intimate level, who were intrigued by the seeming magic of the world of music performance.

The concentration was intense, the air was electric, the music was incredibly beautiful and the music-making was intoxicating, as we had the opportunity to work in close proximity for up to 20 hours a day. It is a world that many, as adults, wish they may have experienced but never had the opportunity to do so, and it was a privilege to have the ability to transcend to a space of complete freedom of sound that allowed me to sing unhindered for hours on end.

I was not a name in lights, but you have to be good to be offered such highly competitive roles in Europe. You also have to be consistent and have nerves of steel. In the end, this was both my failing and then my driving force to help others (I am reminded of the ancient phrase 'physician, heal thyself'). And it also prompted my move away from performing and towards the corporate world.

In retrospect, the initial move for me from a career in singing opera to the corporate world may have appeared to be uncharacteristically heading in the wrong direction. But in reality, the lessons learned in one were just what I needed to help bring me to where I needed to be.

The Lessons of Opera

What I recall in retrospect were the skills of conductors who, although never making a sound, inspired others to rousing performances.

I remember the breathless shock of hearing international pianist Murray Perahia playing the introduction of a Mozart aria and being silenced by the beauty of his touch.

I remember discussing (and rehearsing) the importance of a millisecond pause in the music with Ian Burnside before a performance and practising the coordination of breath as we began a recital.

I remember Heather Harper's incredible agility and body strength, and Galina Vishnevskaya's magic as she wove evocative tales around us with her vivid imagination.

I experienced singers bringing a complete audience of several thousand people to tears. Although they stood on the stage, appearing as prima donnas (with an aura of self-interest), they were acutely aware of their effect on the audience, their coordination with the many other players on stage and the technical requirements of the staging, not to mention the music and emotion of the particular aria.

I was particularly fascinated by some famous names, who achieved these results with virtually no rehearsal, meeting their co-singers for the first time as they appeared in the spotlight. To actually pull off such a feat and produce a magnificent performance, true to themselves, to the music, to their audience, was something that was achieved through years of constant work and discipline.

Eventually, I brought these learnings with me, out of the world of opera and into the world of communication. I knew the world of discipline of performance, of excellence, of imbuing respect and trust, and this, I realised, was a legacy from the world of ancient Greek and Roman gravitas.

A Niche

My unique lens and perspective gave me new insight into the world of leadership and emerging leadership communication. This is where I have found my niche: working with intelligent leaders and emerging leaders who struggle with communication, confidence and imposter syndrome (that uncomfortable feeling you get when you think you're unqualified and incompetent). All that these leaders are missing—all that they need to truly realise their potential and create real impact—is the right set of skills.

Of course, leaving the world of opera for the corporate world meant starting from scratch, translating the gifts from that 'other world' into the present one, guided by the lessons from my different lens and the ancients.

I got a job at what was then Australia's largest company, quickly becoming part of the state-wide management team. Working with corporate executives, I witnessed how many of them expressed themselves in a dry, seemingly emotionless manner.

One day in Switzerland years previously, I had spent maybe 10 hours straight with Dame Elisabeth Schwarzkopf focusing on the amount of air to escape on two notes in an aria from the opera *Der Rosenkavalier*. Now, at work, I found myself dumbstruck listening to an executive stand in front of his group with no projection and a nasal drone. I thought to myself: 'What strategy are you using here, mate?' I just couldn't believe anyone could be so out of tune with their sound, which was such a stark contrast to the focus on voice and communication that I'd been used to.

And so the journey began. Applying my performance training, I began to consider that face-to-face presentations consisted of information 'dumps', based almost exclusively on a combination of two approaches: aggressive confrontation and stifling mono-tonality. The communication was generally either blunt and aggressive, or poorly structured and dull.

In 30 years in the corporate world, I've seen that the field of corporate leadership in Australia has gone through intense external pressure to develop catalysts that help leaders change an organisation. Those catalysts are at least partly achievable through honed interpersonal skills, including dialogue and 'inspirational speech making'.[1] But there was and still is a gap in the skill of delivery. Delivery is not just a component of communication: it's a way of working on the speaker's connection with self. It's how leaders connect authentically with their people.

And decades later, the need is bottomless. Results from the 2023 Edelman Trust Barometer show negative progress and an ever-downwards spiral of leadership presence and the perception of trust by others.[2]

What my experiences in the performance sphere have taught me is that in many cases, the elements wholly embraced by the singing and performing professions precisely mirror what is missing in the way leaders struggle to communicate effectively today.

In singing, we studied languages voraciously—looking at each word, the literal meaning of the sentence, the overall meaning of the sentence, the linguistics and the flow of the sentence—and then devised ways to match the pitch and the emotion. We studied the composition of a score and rehearsed. There was a focus on scenery, on lighting, on stage movement, on body flexibility and on working with others, and then there was even more rehearsal. The focus for change was on direct, immediate responses, and there was a constant recognition of the need to battle the unconscious mind to facilitate transformation. This was about building trust in our sound and respect for every aspect of what was conveyed. This was gravitas.

But how could I instil these skills in those wishing to communicate with others when the profession and language of opera seemed so distant from everyday needs?

And then, like a gift from the heavens, I discovered Cicero, Quintilian and many other ancient scholars. The adage 'everything old is new again' seemed to ring true. Reading their work was like music to my ears, seeing that literally everything they said supported everyday communication as a performance art. Their work describes and differentiates the work towards gravitas through Aristotle's five canons of rhetoric and provides practical, applicable and immediately accessible skills.

Here was a formula. Here was a deep understanding. The millennia have not dulled the relevance of the ancient experts. Here is everything we need to move forward in today's world.

INTRODUCTION

Donald Trump prepares to enter the stage at the National Golf Club in Bedminster, New Jersey, following his arraignment in Miami. He had entered a not guilty plea to 37 counts related to allegations that he kept hundreds of classified documents after his term of office expired.[1]

Back in New Jersey, the gathered throng are at a fever pitch when a loud, deep voice announces (a presupposition that is a stretch, at best): 'Ladies and gentlemen. The next President of the United States!' The audience, coaxed by a core of vocal leaders, are transfixed as they chant together 'USA! USA! USA!' Trump finally enters, stops in the middle of the doorway, and gestures with his arms open wide and hands facing forwards. Behind him, the flags of the nation provide a superb photographic opportunity.

Whether you like Trump or not is a personal opinion (this is certainly not a book about politics!), but it is undeniable that when he is on stage, the whole event is choreographed around his delivery. He is able to profoundly influence those in his audience, having received an astounding 67.87 million votes in 2020, nearly five million more than in 2016.[2] And while his theatrics are unusual in today's political and leadership world, their overwhelming impact fascinates (or infuriates) an audience across the globe (despite the somewhat confusing and unclear speeches he often makes alongside his delivery!).

The long and the short of it…Trump has some form of gravitas. The question about whether he uses this skill with moral fortitude is a separate one. (Tiro, the assistant of Cicero, is imagined by Robert Harris to have quoted Cicero in his dying words to have said, 'Power brings a man many luxuries, but a clean pair of hands is seldom amongst them.'[3]) And the answer is not obvious.

My question to you is this: can we leave the influencing to those who may not have the best intentions, when those who do are struggling?

And of course, we should take courage from the fact that—when it comes to gravitas—even the bravest fall.

The famous British-American journalist and award-winning film-maker Louis Theroux once interviewed British adventurer, writer and television personality Bear Grylls. In this absorbing interview,[4] Grylls talks about his incredible feats of bravery and survival. But he also mentions that when it comes to presenting to an audience, he crumbles. Despite being able to eat spiders and scale mountains, when it came to public speaking Grylls said, 'I hate this more than anything.'

So what's the difference between his epic survival struggles and speaking with kids? Well, when it comes to his physical feats of endurance and bravery, he has catchphrases, rituals and techniques that help him to manage all the obstacles he faces, whether they're planned or unplanned. However, when it comes to presenting to a large group, he has nothing. Guided by a chasm of nothingness, his unconscious mind takes control and he is left scrambling.

As Bear Grylls' experience shows, many people are in this position—even the bravest among us. But why? Why are we struggling?

Communication and Confidence

The way we currently communicate has left many people—speakers and listeners alike—with a lack of confidence. This is not an innate lack. It is a gaping hole in our training. And while we were not doing well before COVID-19, the predominance of virtual communication has highlighted a weakness that is leading to disassociation, isolation and imposter syndrome. We sit quietly at the end of a virtual call, struggling to engage, absorb or respond to information because we've never been taught how to communicate better, and we believe, through experience and by watching those who came before us, that this is what's expected. When we're the ones communicating, we too often lack structure and organisation, and we tend to overlook the missing skills of delivery that would enhance our communication, instead focused on reading from a scrappy piece of paper.

With around 75 per cent of people having glossophobia[5] (the fear of public speaking), one of the biggest challenges for those in the workplace is to have the confidence to speak publicly and communicate with excellence. An apparent lack of confidence in the speaker, which leads to a crumpled posture, blocked voice and a propensity to waffle, can, in turn, lead the audience to experience a lack of respect and trust in the speaker. Lack of confidence also has a direct link to performance anxiety and imposter syndrome, which can lead to us doubting our own talents and feeling like we don't deserve our role or our success. And both of these have been magnified post-COVID. The pressure has never been greater, and the skills have never been more wanting.

What is it that's holding us back from having the confidence to speak well in public and communicating with excellence—whether that's to a small room of colleagues, or on a large stage? It's the feeling that we lack gravitas. It's the feeling that we don't have the skills to deliver in a way that aligns with our authenticity as a speaker or thinker, and in a way that reinforces our authority and builds trust with our audience.

But we can build this confidence, create trust and authority and, ultimately, build our own gravitas. And to do this, we start with the learning of the ancients.

Learnings from the Ancients

These communication and confidence challenges need solutions, but there's no need to recreate the wheel. The solution does not lie in mindset: it comes from action. The answers lie in tangible, useful and immediately applicable skills of delivery, like those used by the ancient Greeks and Romans. These were people devoted to oratory and the trust and respect known as gravitas, which required a lifetime of constant application to achieve excellence.

But today we find a world where one of the key elements of rhetoric, delivery, has been completely overlooked. Delivery is where our communications fall down. And to develop gravitas we must bring delivery back into the way we speak, work and lead others.

The question arises as to why we have not recognised the ancients' knowledge of gravitas before. One explanation is that the skills are difficult to describe on paper, and so the solutions appear to have rotted on the shelves.

To reinstate the skill of delivery, we must:

- shatter the paradigms that have led to our current outdated and ineffective model of communication

- reinstate the body as the core of delivery (and therefore communication)

- reintroduce voice into the equation

- re-engage gestures in our communication

- look at the modern frameworks of rhetoric (and what's missing)

- actively practise the skills of rhetoric.

Much of what we need to do to achieve this, and solve today's modern crisis of communication, has already been developed. We just need to know where to look. And this book will show you how!

A Different Lens

The ancients believed that confidence is a choice and is gained by taking action. It's time we re-learned how their knowledge can be used to bridge our modern gaps in communication and confidence. In this book, you'll discover a new model of communication, built on that timeless wisdom. It's a model that anyone can implement, easily, in their own lives, and gain back those feelings of confidence and trust that are so vital to communicating well.

In this book, you'll discover that our actions are a set of habitual patterns, as opposed to the idea that somebody is 'a natural' or has a 'good voice'. I focus on three major areas of new skills—body, gestures and voice—which can help you to, ultimately, achieve your goal of learning gravitas.

This model is built on the following principles:

- Each person is born with a perfect instrument (body and voice).

- All people can express themselves.

- There are no bad sounds, although sometimes there are unhealthy sounds.

- Voice, body and mind are inextricably linked.

In Roman times, reputedly the greatest orator of all time, Marcus Tullius Cicero (106–43 BCE), was what was called a *novus homo*, a 'new man', with the handicap of no family or famous ancestors. This meant he had no role models to look to who could share the skills with him that he needed for his future. But Cicero knew how to grow. He understood the notion of developing skills and habitual change and learnt to 'play his own body'.

This was the skills development he experienced, and the skills development I experienced during my opera study. These experiences have shaped the method I have developed to help people in the workplace create stronger communications and leadership today.

How to Use This Book

My mission in this book is not to influence you about politics (Trump) or send you out into the wilderness (like Grylls)! It is also *not* a fulsome, in-depth exploration of rhetoric and gravitas. If you're a rhetorician or interested in a deep dive into the full research and studies, both ancient and contemporary, around this subject, get in touch—I'd be happy to send you my PhD work instead!

What this book *is* for is to demonstrate and analyse the techniques used by those who are experts at influence, including those scholars of ancient Greece and Rome—who showcase that quality of gravitas—and explore the research (both modern and ancient) that is applicable to all of us who want to develop those qualities ourselves.

Gravitas will help you to have more confidence in yourself and, in turn, gain more trust and 'buy in' from your audiences. Which means the rewards are substantial.

This book will help you rediscover those skills that lead to the outcomes you're looking for in your communications. It is designed to lay out those solutions so that you can get in tune with better communications, see through the different lens I hope to share and build your own unique gravitas.

Is This Book for You?

While running speaking and coaching events, I hear over and over how people struggle to communicate confidently. This book is for you if you're worried that your voice is not being heard in the workplace (or in life), that you lack gravitas, or that your communication is weak and ineffectual. And if you are feeling this way, it's important to understand that you're not alone.

But great news ... there are practical tools you can apply to overcome this struggle, and they're right here in this book!

Let's get started!

Chapter 1

Gravitas

Joan came to me three years ago in a state of complete distress. She had an important position as a thought leader in her field and had been asked some time ago to present at a major conference.

This was an important occasion for her. It represented the culmination of years of work and demonstrated how she was now being appreciated by her community. She felt pressure to showcase her thinking and leverage her success, while at the same time being humble—all the while delivering a presentation that would leave the audience captivated and motivated.

Unfortunately, when she walked out on stage to deliver her presentation, she saw the audience and froze. She was struck with a tremendous case of performance anxiety.

After mumbling a few words, sweating, losing all the moisture in her mouth and fumbling, she left the stage. No one knew what to say. No one wanted to speak to her. She went home and her journey with performance anxiety began … until we met.

Today, after our work together on communication and gravitas, Joan speaks to thousands internationally. She is a key thought leader in her field, and she is seen and heard as such. She is able to lead with gravitas—and if it works for Joan, it can work for you.

Understanding how to lead with gravitas begins with understanding what gravitas is, and how it works together with the terms *oratory* (the art or practice of speaking in public) and *rhetoric* (the art or practice of persuasive speech or writing).

Our modern understanding of these ideas has changed significantly from the way they were originally understood by the ancient Romans and Greeks, and I believe that we have much to learn from them. By investigating this ancient understanding we can learn not only how to better understand gravitas, but also how to implement it in our lives and our work.

Oratory, Gravitas and Rhetoric

Entering the world of corporate communications, I quickly realised that I needed to rediscover the skills of communication from a fresh perspective. Ultimately, I found this perspective through the learnings of the philosophers and orators of ancient Rome and Greece. But diving into the communication styles of the ancient world was like diving into a can of worms—confusing, wriggly and hard to pin down!

From my opera background, I knew that our modern way of communicating—particularly in relation to being able to communicate with gravitas—was simply not working well. But I believed that what we were missing had already been discovered and that it had existed in ancient Greece and Rome. Somehow, it had become lost—and I believe that we need to bring this back into our modern-day communications. My task is to unearth these skills and redefine the possibilities. And to do that we need to first clarify what we mean by oratory, rhetoric and gravitas.

Understanding Oratory

'Oratory' means the art or practice of speaking in public. While the permutations and combinations of methods of public speaking are endless, we have come to associate oratory today with effective and skilful public speaking, but the story of what we understand oratory to be begins with the ancient Greeks.

The first Greek-speaking tribes entered Greece during the late Bronze Age, around 1800 BCE.[1] The practice known as oratory began with these tribes and went on to flourish during the late 400s and the 300s BCE.[2]

One of the earliest Greek orators was Lysias (445–380 BCE, approximately). As well as being an orator himself, he was highly sought after as a speechmaker. He was well known for delivering speeches that were simple and direct, and the speeches he created for others—particularly those who were defending themselves in courts (or in the court of public opinion)—were brilliantly tailored to the person delivering the speech, helping to make them appear more likeable and their message more persuasive. With the reference to speech 'delivery', I found what I believe has been missing from our current understanding of gravitas and communicating with gravitas. The evolution of my understanding of gravitas began to take shape.

As opposed to the simple style of Lysias, the great orator Demosthenes (384–322 BCE) was known for his grand, stately style. Another famous Greek orator, Aeschines (389–314 BCE), favoured speeches that contained vivid descriptions rather than relying on persuasive logic.

In ancient Greece, orators' speeches were often compared to theatrical performances. Excellent orators wouldn't just say the words; they would use gestures, body movements and, of course, the stage itself to deliver their words to the audience and enhance the speech's message. This hints at the incredible breadth of opportunity to express one's individual style when speaking or communicating, an element that was embraced by these early orators.

As global power moved from ancient Greece to ancient Rome, most Roman citizens would eventually need to call upon these public speaking skills—either during public meetings or when taking part in court cases. So the educational focus was designed to produce skilled orators who could deliver speeches before the people, in the courts and even before the Roman Senate.

Students of oratory would learn how to select the subject matter for their speeches and how to compose the speech itself, particularly how to influence their audience. They were taught to utilise both logic and emotion to draw the listeners to their own side. Students of rhetoric and oratory learned how to select appropriate subjects for their speeches and how to influence their listeners by appealing to their sense of logic and to their emotions.[3] They also learned other subjects—like literature, mythology, philosophy, geography and even music—to support their future orations.[4]

Students were also taught different styles of speechmaking—which could be simple and direct or grandiose and overblown—and the best time to use those different styles. They were taught memory devices they could use when delivering long speeches to help them remember their main points. They also studied various techniques to create effective speeches, including gestures and dramatic uses of the voice.[5]

This educational focus created generations of skilled orators who could argue before the law courts, before the Senate and before the people as a whole. Trust and respect were key, confidence was essential to oratory success, and it all came from years of devoted study and ongoing practice.

The rise and fall of oratory

Anciently, oratory had broader connotations than effective and skilful public speaking. The point of oratory was to deal with ignorance, bring about like-mindedness and motivate action.[6] Aristotle (384–322 BCE), the ancient Greek philosopher, scientist and intellectual, defined three types of oratory:

1. **Judicial oratory.** Courtroom speeches that primarily focused on describing and opining on past events.

2. **Deliberative oratory.** A public debate or discussion about the best course of action to take on any given subject. In this case, orators would attempt to convince listeners to come round to their way of thinking or to align with their opinion.

3. **Epideictic oratory.** Also known as 'display speeches', orators delivered these speeches primarily to show off their skills. They were typically centred around praising or blaming someone—perhaps easy topics to create a strong display of oratory, as they allowed for the opportunity to raise passions and encourage identification (whether towards the positive or away from the negative). Funeral orations were also considered a type of epideictic oratory.[7]

So why did oratory lose favour in around 300 CE? I believe there are several reasons.

1. EMPERORS GAINED ABSOLUTE POWER

Over time, oratory began to lose its power in the ancient world. In Rome it was still important, but primarily as a form of entertainment in social occasions, rather than as a method of public discourse. One reason for this was that during the Roman Empire, emperors gained absolute power, so oratory was no longer required (or accepted) as a political tool.

Still, ancient Roman orators remained models of excellence, and students continued to study the great speeches and speechmakers as models of the power of language.

2. DOCUMENTATION WAS SCANT OR LOST

Much of the work around the physical elements of oration has been lost. While we think of Aristotle as a great reference, this is only partly true. His influence was more in the area of the canon of 'arrangement', leaving the discussion of delivery to other experts, whose works did not survive from the time. And Aristotle never claimed to be a source of all elements of rhetoric, with some claiming he was even dismissive of delivery,[8] considering it vulgar and important only because of 'the corruption of the hearer'. (I cover the five canons of rhetoric, including arrangement and delivery, later in this chapter.)

The truth, however, is that Aristotle considered delivery 'of the greatest importance,'[9] but without the works of others to fill the gaps, this has left us in the dark, in terms of understanding how to use oratory today.

We do have some works from the ancients remaining. The most fulsome and helpful for us in modern times is Marcus Fabius Quintilianus's *Institutio Oratoria*.[10] Colloquially known as 'Quintilian' (35–96 CE), he was a Roman educator and well-known persuasive speaker, and this book continues to be our most useful source on the nonverbal elements of oratory.

6

Quintilian noted that gestures could convey meaning without words. He believed they constituted an entire language that an orator must master and could use to supplement his control of words.[11] He delved into that world more deeply than any other ancient work that remains with us today.

A few other works remain as well, and their attitude is best exemplified by an anecdote that Cicero, Quintilian and nearly every other commentator on oratory repeated concerning Demosthenes, the greatest Greek orator. When asked to list the three most important elements of oratory, Demosthenes replied that delivery was the single most important element of great oratory (effectively, his response was 'delivery, delivery, delivery'!).[12]

While much of the ancients' work in this area has been lost, the subject of nonverbal oratory has also not then been addressed by any modern rhetorical treatise. There is much discussion around Roman rhetoric in general, but the detail is never explored—for example, even in the 700 pages of the bestselling leadership and communications treatise *The Articulate Executive*, only 20 pages are devoted to delivery methodologies, such as gestures, voice and body movements.[13] This hardly reflects the emphasis or importance spoken about by Demosthenes.

3. CHRISTIANITY MOVED IN A DIFFERENT DIRECTION

One of the tenets of being a follower of Christ was the requirement to speak honestly and plainly. In his book *On Christian Doctrine*, Saint Augustine (354–430 CE) says, 'Eloquent speakers give pleasure, wise ones salvation.'[14]

During research for my PhD, I visited church leaders to discuss their oratory skills. Almost without exception those leaders told me that there was no conscious programme, but instead they were 'channelled by God'. I know God is good, but it might be asking a lot of God to be so attentive every time a pastor stands to speak. It is my contention that many of the skills religious leaders demonstrate are actually skills of oratory embodied thousands of years hence and, over the years, passed down from generation to generation through watching and experiencing the skills of the past generations. In other words, they may not 'study' oratory, but they learn how to persuade and emotively engage through the same skills that the ancients would have used, which are taught to them in the seminary or from more senior leaders. But maybe that's just me being the sceptic!

Anciently, the Christians denounced oratory as a field of study—instead implying that they relied solely on God to speak through them—and as they soon held sway over the education of the masses, this meant that oratory fell out of favour.[15] The rise of Christianity didn't spell the end of rhetoric and oratory completely; however, it did move the study and focus of both areas from the political (or secular) world and into the religious world with the closing of the Platonic (secular) schools in around 529 BCE.[16]

Those interested in the role of rhetoric were no longer focused on winning court cases or persuading an audience to their own political ends. Instead, they were concerned with winning over the souls of the listeners to Christianity through preaching, sermons and letter writing.[17]

Around 1000 BCE, teaching and learning moved into cathedral schools (designed almost exclusively for the children of wealthy families who were often being prepared for a life in the church).[18] Because of the Crusades, ancient texts started to be rediscovered, which led to the revival of the liberal arts, including what was known as the 'Trivium' (grammar, rhetoric and logic) and the 'Quadrivium' (arithmetic, mathematics, astronomy and geometry).[19]

The 13th century saw the rise of Catholic-funded universities. These institutions began to gather and compile the ancient texts and study them in an effort to improve their preaching and religious communications. And while this was a departure from the way rhetoric was used by the ancients, it did serve the important purpose of preserving those texts for our use today.

4. THE MODES OF DELIVERY CHANGED

Mark Wollacott, a writer and expert in humanities and language with a fascination for the wisdom of the ancients, defines the focus on rhetoric as opposed to oratory. He says, 'Both oratory and rhetoric are deeply connected. This is because, in older times, oratory was the only means of delivering rhetoric.'[20]

Ancient orators didn't have the widespread dissemination of information that we have today. They had to use the systems of the time—which were public orations delivered to the people directly.

But over time this began to change. The first Roman postal service was established in 14 CE. Moveable type was invented by the Chinese around 1041, which allowed for the widespread printing of books for mass distribution. And around 1605, a German publisher, Johann Carolus, printed and distributed the world's first newspaper.[21]

People today can publish their thoughts in newspapers or books, and they can spread their ideas via radio spots, on television and through digital means, such as articles, podcasts or even on social media. Because of this ability to reach out to our audience in a myriad of ways, the belief that we need the skills of public orators has waned and almost disappeared. And we've been left the worse off for it.

Understanding Rhetoric

As we have seen, today the lines between what is rhetoric and what is not have become blurred. Aristotle, our primary source for the canons of rhetoric, focused on his areas of expertise, leaving us wanting in the area of delivery (which though important, as we'll see, wasn't where Aristotle himself focused his energy). But when we look at the broader picture and see how the ancients really understood (and delivered!) rhetoric and oratory, we can learn so much that can lead us towards better communication (and communicating with gravitas!). So what can we find?

Aristotle defined 'rhetoric' as speech or writing that is intended to persuade people to agree with their way of thinking. As oratory was, in Aristotle's time, the only means of performing rhetoric, it shared the same persuasive purpose.[22] And traditionally, an orator would master all the canons of rhetoric in order to become an effective public speaker.

Aristotle developed the basics of a system of rhetoric — the five canons of rhetoric. These five elements — invention, arrangement, style, memory and delivery[23] — 'thereafter served as the touchstone' of the discipline of rhetoric[24] and have influenced how we've communicated, and studied communication, from ancient through to modern times.

The five canons of rhetoric

The five canons of rhetoric as identified by Aristotle are invention, arrangement, style, memory and delivery. Often these are called the five 'canons' or 'pillars' of rhetoric.

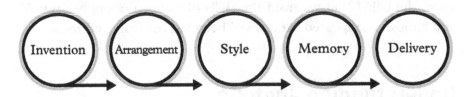

While Aristotle names these the five canons of rhetoric, I believe they can be considered to be the five skills of attaining gravitas.

SKILL 1: INVENTION

Invention is the process of coming up with the material that you're going to use in your speech. It includes naming and developing your message, as well as the factors that make it true or plausible so that you can make a convincing case to the audience. Many people think of this as the brainstorming stage of rhetoric because that is certainly part of the skill of invention.

An example of this in practice is the process of mind mapping. To prepare a speech, you might sit down with paper and start diagramming thoughts, words, concepts, ideas and any other items around a central subject or message. There's no strong organisation here. Using a non-linear layout, the person will end up building in bubbles, frameworks and themes that start to turn into a colourful ideas map that aligns with how your brain and thoughts naturally work.

In the work I do with leaders, the area of 'invention' is generally believed to be a given. So often people sit before me and explain that they know their topic and have no issue with finding material to draw from, which renders the skill of invention as unnecessary. In other words, they think that they know everything there is to know.

On the other hand, I take it as a given all leaders and experts experience the continual need to update their knowledge.

> *For without the consciousness of such preliminary study, our powers of speaking extempore will give us nothing but an empty flow of words, springing from the lips and not from the brain.*[25]
>
> — Quintilian

Whether you feel you have enough subject matter expertise or not, it's important to continue to gain more and more. Suggested modes of improvement are to:

- read good books

- read a lot of books

- read dictionaries

- read aloud to yourself

- use your expertise daily so it remains up to date and relevant.

SKILL 2: ARRANGEMENT

The arrangement is essentially the structure of the oration. This skill involves organising your arguments to give sense and order to your message. A clear and logical arrangement allows you to deliver a coherent oration that your listeners can easily follow and understand.

Arranging your oration generally involves creating an outline that sets out the order in which you'll deliver your major points. You'll typically start with introducing your subject, then move onto the points that support your thesis. Ensuring that these points make logical sense and that they also transition smoothly is one of the most important aspects of your arrangement.

Elements I see as critical in arrangements today are:

- **The notion of three.**[26] Known in ancient times as *'omne trium perfectum'* — or 'everything that is three is perfect', this tenet can inform the arrangement of your messages. For example, the national motto of France is liberty, equality, and fraternity. So, if you were a French politician, you might develop a speech around these three central ideas.

- **The three proofs for the inventor.** These 'proofs' are ethos, pathos and logos (authority, emotion and logic). When delivering any presentation or speech, you'll use ethos (authority) to establish your credibility, pathos (emotions) to engage with your audience and logos (logic) to authenticate your message.

- **The three questions.** Considering these three essential questions helps give everyone the comfort to move on knowing who (both you and them) is in the room and what you're all trying to achieve. Psychologically, these points need to be handled for the audience to feel rapport.

  a. **Who am I?** This gets to the heart of what kind of expert you are, and where your strengths lie. For example, if you're a team leader in the aerospace field, you might have expertise in your field, but also have experience in team dynamics. Both of these are strengths you can focus on in your presentation.

  For example: 'For those who do not know me, my expertise is in the area of aerospace with experience in team dynamics.'

  b. **Who are they?** This helps you to understand your audience so that you can deliver a message that speaks to their needs. For example, if you're delivering to your team you might engage differently than if you're delivering a speech to a large group of industry professionals.

For example: 'It is an honour to be here with such an esteemed group of experts in your field, who have travelled from all areas of the country to be here for your annual conference.'

c. **What am I trying to tell them?** This helps you to clarify the main point of the message that you're looking to communicate. If your goal is to help your immediate team collaborate better, understanding this will help to guide your entire presentation.

For example: 'Our purpose here today is to come together and experience the power of team collaboration.'

SKILL 3: STYLE

Style is including and adapting suitable words and sentences within your speech to suit your audience. Style also encompasses tone. You'll want to choose how professional or accessible you want to be. You'll want to consider whether you want to be direct and simple or more grandiose, and whether you want to use humour or stories (and I recommend both!).

Much of your style will depend on both your platform (are you on a stage in front of 500 people or in a team meeting of 10?) and your audience. Depending on those factors, you'll want to change up your style to best suit.

When I do breakfast television, the simplest of words are broken down by the interviewers. They know their audience and any long and seldom-used words are pulled up immediately and translated and questioned further. It drives me to drink, but at the same time I question whether I am trying to show off by wearing the cloak of the intellectual, which impresses no one in that environment. In fact, in the end they want to laugh and learn something new. It's not about me.

In every case you need to ensure that your style doesn't overshadow or convolute your message. Steer clear of complicated ideas and jargon, or anything else that will confuse (and lose) your audience. Use metaphors and storytelling as part of your process as this aids in delivering a clear and memorable message. When someone can easily understand you, it builds credibility and therefore trust.

SKILL 4: MEMORY

Memory is the firm retention in the mind of the message, words and arrangement, and the steps that you take to recall the main points of your message. This is not about making your speech memorable to others, but about the skill of remembering the elements of your presentation overall.

We aren't generally taught the skills of memory today, and many of my clients don't know where to begin when remembering their content. Lack of sleep, stress and overwork will put pressure on your cognitive skills, so having great techniques to help you retain information is essential.

It's important to recognise that memory is not a shoebox you fill, then once it is full, no more can be put inside. Instead, memory is like a muscle. You can grow it and strengthen it over time with practice and use.

I have found that when you are memorising a speech it is best to memorise the outline of the talk rather than the talk verbatim. This allows you to hit all the main points of your message, while still permitting the freedom of natural flow and responsiveness.

SKILL 5: DELIVERY

The final canon or skill of rhetoric is delivery. In the simplest terms, delivery is the process of presenting your ideas to an audience. But, in practice, delivery involves so much more.

Delivery was known in ancient Greece and Rome as the graceful regulation of voice, countenance and gestures. In fact, Quintilian tells us, 'Delivery is by most writers called action, but it appears to derive the one name from the voice and the other from the gesture.'[27] He goes on to qualify that 'delivery in general … depends upon two things, voice and gesture, of which the one affects the eyes and the other the ears'.[28] The ancients knew that in perfecting our delivery we had to think both about our voice—how we sound and speak—and our bodies. This includes our movements and gestures, and where we hold our hands—and even how we stand. Unfortunately, though this was integral to what the ancients knew about delivery and oration, it was lost over time.

As the Cambridge-educated economist and scholar Sylvia Ann Hewlett tells us, 'Among modern scholars, oratorical delivery has been somewhat neglected as a topic of enquiry, but to the ancients it was of vital interest.'[29]

The twist

Here is where the twist begins—where oration becomes divorced from the element of delivery, and we lose the vital element that drives gravitas. Although Aristotle defined the five canons of rhetoric, he was clear that his work focused on words and language, which was separate to delivery. Without that focus—and without the work of other ancient scholars to bolster our understanding of delivery—over time, the pillars of rhetoric have become confused.

I put it to you that the 'skills of oratory' we know today combine only the pillars of arrangement and style. They sideline invention and memory and ignore delivery (or treat delivery in the most banal way). Sylvia Ann Hewlett's observation that delivery is 'somewhat neglected' is, in fact, an understatement. Delivery has been virtually abandoned.

Evidence of this can be found in modern university programmes and the supporting literature.

In the US, the University of Utah describes its rhetoric programme as one that teaches students how 'culture and society shape what we define as "literacy".' Students who choose to study rhetoric at the U of U can 'choose courses from topics such as under-represented rhetorics, rhetorics of gender, writing popular non-fiction, professional discourse, grammar and stylistics, digital storytelling and writing as a social practice'.[30]

In Europe, the Catholic University in Leuven notes that its course in rhetoric is linked to other introductory courses, 'such as "Critical Text Analysis" in the Master of Journalism, and "Speech Analysis" in the Master in Interpreting.'[31]

A more thorough examination of the coursework does nothing to dispel this understanding. There is no hint here of the skills of delivery or memorisation. These skills are left wanting.

Wollacott says: 'Part of what separates oratory and rhetoric is that oratory requires the speaker to have a natural skill set, including charm and charisma as well as a good voice.'[32] However, I beg to differ. I believe our current mindset on delivery is not looking through the lens of possible change when we accept Wollacott's statement about 'a natural skill set' and 'a good voice'.

As an expert in this field, I can tell you we can all have 'good' voices. We do not require a 'natural skill set'. To get to a house of international opera as a girl from what is satirically known as 'Brisvegas' was not a result of my innate talent. The ancient Romans who worked daily on their skills were not divided out because of 'natural talent'. It is my understanding and experience, reinforced by the literature, that voice is a learned skill that must be practised and polished over time.

I suggest that of the five canons of rhetoric, which I see today as the five skills of oratory, postulated by Aristotle, the percentages attributed to each today is as follows.

However, to really embrace our ability to lead with gravitas, we have to shift these percentages closer to what the ancients originally believed. That is, we need to add much greater weight to the skill of delivery.

Re-focus on delivery

A poor speech accompanied by great delivery is better than a great speech accompanied by poor delivery.[33]

— Quintilian

One of the primary elements of our new model of communication is the focus on delivery. Think of Jacinda Ardern, a leader I believe turned the tables with her expressions of emotion and seemingly honest outpourings about events that stunned the world. Analysing Jacinda, you see that her voice of empathy is exceptional, her use of touch is world-leading and her attention to structure and message outstanding, while not appearing obvious in any way. (Please note I am not commenting on her politics, but the way she expresses herself in a leadership role.)

Similarly, Volodymyr Zelenskyy, the President of Ukraine, has astounded the world with his poise in communication under enormous stress. It is no surprise to me that Zelenskyy is a trained actor and comedian: these skills come in handy! And yes, it is still totally authentic.

The question is, how do we make our delivery interesting and also professional? The answer is not as difficult as you might think. Over many years, I have seen those who work with me on the skills of gravitas see the light of hope and go from believing that gravitas is something you either have or don't have, to something that can be learned and developed with understanding and hard work. And once they learn that they can never go back to that comatose state.

However, to make swift progress on this journey—to speed up the transition from unbelieving and unskilled speakers to believing and skilled speakers who deliver with gravitas—it is necessary to refocus on delivery, elevating it from its neglected, abandoned state to one of the most important skills of oratory overall.

Let's return for a moment to all five canons or skills of rhetoric. Of course invention remains important. But, as leaders, emerging leaders and those who are experts in a field often tell me, their knowledge of their topic is excellent. We might need to keep perhaps a 5 per cent focus on invention in order to keep our knowledge fresh.

Arrangement also continues to be important as we need to learn the frameworks for the various scenarios we face today, such as a television interview, a conference representation, presenting your idea in the boardroom or handling a difficult situation. So, perhaps we need to allow a 15 per cent focus on arrangement.

For the other two components, style and memory, we might need to allocate 5 per cent of effort to style and considering the appropriate language, and 15 per cent on memory. This means we can take our carefully planned words from the written form to the audience without relying on notes.

Finally, we can invest the remaining proportion of our time and energy on delivery, which really does demand about 60 per cent of our focus.

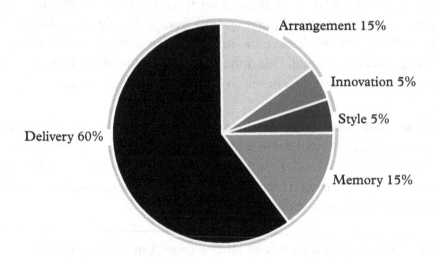

This model is influenced by the writing of Demosthenes, who, when asked about the three most important elements 'in the whole art of oratory', said that delivery is the first, second and third most important element.[34] In other words, he believed it was the single most important part of oratory.

Cicero believed delivery has the 'sole and supreme power in oratory'.[35] Further, Quintilian said: 'For my own part, I should be inclined to say that language of but moderate merit, recommended by a forcible delivery, will make more impression than the very best if it is unattended with that advantage.'[36]

It's in the delivery that we are really able to embrace the elements that allow us to be individuals that can communicate with gravitas.

Understanding Gravitas

Working through the five canons of rhetoric, one achieves gravitas—the manner of trust and respect. It encompasses all the five pillars of rhetoric—but mainly 'delivery'.

Gravitas is variously defined as 'dignity, seriousness or solemnity of manner',[37] 'high seriousness'[38] and 'seriousness and importance of manner, causing feelings of respect and trust in others'.[39] As you can see, the main thrust here is one of seriousness.

Anciently, *gravitas* was also understood to embody several complementary attributes of moral rigor and absolute commitment to the task at hand. But there is something missing in today's definition that the ancients understood.

The Romans lived by a set of virtues. These were the qualities of life to which every citizen aspired. They were at the heart of the *Via Romana*—the Roman Way—and are thought to be those qualities that gave the Roman Republic the moral strength to conquer and civilise the world.

Of those virtues, there were three foundational virtues. These were *pietas* (piety), *dignitas* (dignity) and *gravitas*. These three formed the basis for the expression of all other essential virtues, the most important of these being that beyond all else, the person must be 'good'.[40]

'I hold that no one can be a true orator unless he is also a good man and even if he could be, I would not have it so.'[41]

— Quintilian

Unfortunately, there is no contemporaneous work specifically focused on describing or examining these virtues. Modern scholars assume that these ideals were so ingrained in the culture and society of the time that formal exploration was hardly necessary.[42]

As part of this trio of foundational virtues that called for a public persona—and in this case, the ancient Romans meant a male persona—that would be serious, dignified and proper within the perimeters defined by society, gravitas was considered absolutely essential to the task of retaining a proper place in the community. Without qualities such as a depth of personality and weighty judgement (which were understood to be fundamental to the virtue of gravitas), a male would often slip to a slightly less desirable position in society, which in turn would adversely impact the standing of his children within the community.

(This constant reference to the male of the species, of course, begs the question as to whether the whole topic is relevant for women. Spoiler alert: the answer is yes!)

A balanced approach

While we associate gravitas today with weight and seriousness, this was never the only intention of the ancient Romans. In fact, during the Roman period they spoke of it as being a balance between weight and levity. This consisted of humour, humility and wit. Perhaps the swing occurred in 1687, when Isaac Newton described gravity as a one-way weighty force. Perhaps not, but somehow we did lose the part of gravitas that embraced levity.

Today, our understanding of 'communication' is limited by our modern definition of communication and our understanding of the foundation term of gravitas. And this confusion has minimised the art of communication.

We have also lost our focus on teaching communication (and therefore, lost our ability to easily harness the elements of gravitas). Here in Australia, we have two schools alone (Curtin and ANU) that study the art of speaking. Focusing on frameworks in the school of journalism, ANU says their education introduces students to the structuring of arguments, and the framing and communication of issues on behalf of government, industry, non-government organisations and individuals.[43]

And we've also incorrectly associated gravitas with some of the most heinous individuals in our history, such as Adolf Hitler, cult leaders and charlatan politicians. We have lost the important notion of 'good' as being part of gravitas. But the skills of gravitas are those that we, as 'good people', must recognise and learn, so that we ourselves can influence others for the better and stop allowing those who may have poor intentions to be the only ones to enjoy this skill.

Is gravitas learnable?

Diagrammatically, I see gravitas as an aura-like factor that exudes from a speaker. We might think of this today as the 'x-factor'. But, unlike the connotations of singing competitions and reality TV, for us the x-factor is not an undefinable skill that comes from innate talent. Instead, gravitas is an absolutely learnable skill that we can all incorporate—men and women, leaders and emerging leaders—be that in business, at rotary events or school meetings.

While Mark Wollacott's musings may imply that gravitas is not learnable, Rebecca Newton, renowned organisational psychologist, on the other hand, believes just the opposite.[44] Like me, she believes that gravitas is learnable and claims that to do so you simply need to:

1. Be clear with yourself about what you want.

2. Be open to feedback.

3. Create time for broader conversations.

While agreeing with Rebecca Newton on gravitas's attainability, I have a strong belief that gravitas involves curating a set of tangible delivery skills that have little to do with 'being open' or 'creating time'. I will be exploring these skills of change in this book.

Summary

In summary, gravitas is the feeling that you evoke that creates respect and trust—for anyone, anywhere and at any time. From my experiences developing the manner of gravitas during my career as a singer, I have come to respect that for anyone communicating with the spoken word, one could not be better guided than to follow the five canons of rhetoric as laid out by Aristotle, and explored further by Quintilian, Cicero and others.

However, we cannot be led astray by the modern-day development of our understanding of rhetoric through university courses as a tool for studying writing. Instead, we need to focus on rhetoric that goes back to the original definition of delivery between individuals one-on-one or to crowds of people. It is delivery that requires the human body and voice to appear and be heard. It is rhetoric where Aristotle's canon of 'delivery' takes centre stage, reinstates gestures, vocal tone and posture, and begins again to build the skills of memory.

This is how we convey confidence, engender trust and demonstrate that vital, day-to-day and, importantly, *leadership* trait of gravitas. It's also what gives us the confidence we need to overcome any performance anxiety.

A New York think tank reported that 67 per cent of senior executives surveyed saw gravitas as the core characteristic of executive presence (which was described as 'the ability to present yourself in a way that signals to the world that you are leadership material').[45] We need gravitas in our political leaders, and we need gravitas in every person who wants to be seen and heard to shape the world for whatever purpose holds value to them.

In other words, to become an effective and inspirational individual in today's world, you must be able to grasp and maintain the element of gravitas. If you're wondering where you can go to learn, you've come to the right place.

Chapter 2

Rethinking the Model of Communication

When it comes to learning a better way to communicate, my experience and subsequent research led me straight back to the ancients. What did the ancient Romans and Greeks know that we don't? What skills did they demonstrate? And what can we bring back to our modern communication today?

Aristotle's Model of Communication

A speaker can no more be eloquent without a large audience than a flute player can perform without a flute.[1]

— Cicero

The ancient Romans and Greeks had a perspective on the audience that may appear unusual today—the audience played an active role in communications.

Cicero's quote gives us our first insight into the ancients' thinking about the role of the audience in communication. In fact, the ancients understood that the audience was as important a part of good communication as the speaker. Whether large or small in size, the audience played a vital role in the effective exchange of ideas.

Aristotle initiated the earliest communication model, which today we call, rather uncreatively, Aristotle's Model of Communication.[2] Like Cicero, Aristotle advocated, firstly, for the speaker to take the responsibility for managing the communication. But secondly (and importantly), he posited that the audience played a critical role in the communication process.

Aristotle's Model of Communication has five primary elements:

1. speaker

2. speech

3. occasion

4. audience

5. effect.

In essence, Aristotle's model advises speakers to build their speeches for different audiences at different times (that is, for different occasions) and to achieve different effects, which requires the audience to take an active part.[3]

A misinterpretation: The linear view of Aristotle's Model of Communication

Today, however, we tend to mistakenly view Aristotle's Model of Communication as a linear model. I agree with the components that modern literature espouses — that is, speaker, speech, occasion, audience and effect. But the linear nature imposed upon the model through modern interpretations requires further consideration.

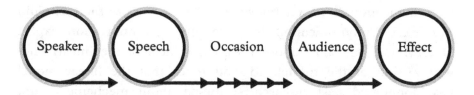

In this linear model, the messages simply flow from the speaker through to the audience. However, anciently these five elements — speaker, speech, occasion, audience and effect — were just that, elements. They were not horizontally laid out in this linear fashion; this was never Aristotle's intention, who simply stated 'of speaker, subject and person addressed — it is the last one, the hearer that determines the speech's end and object'.[4]

The Two-Way Communication of Rome

In ancient times, orations were truly interactive. Together, the speaker and their listeners created dramatic spectacles that included the speaker using the best rhetorical strategies and techniques to arouse the emotions of the audience, and the audience responding with vigorous clapping, humming and chants of praise or criticism. In fact, the interjections and reactions of the audience were incredibly important components of the communication process.

The speaker was certainly responsible for catering their communications for different groups, taking into account different times (occasions) and tailoring for different effects. But to consider it a one-way communication model disregards the responsibilities of the audience.

It is astounding to me that more people haven't expressed surprise at the projection of a linear nature onto Aristotle's Model of Communication. So, I was buoyed to find the work of the Honolulu East-West Communication Institute and communication expert D Lawrence Kincaid,[5] another who is critical of the linear, one-way version of the model. Kincaid notes that the linear model has 'dominated past research', bringing about mechanical (and unsatisfactory) explanations for how to communicate. Instead he suggests 'a paradigm that presents communication as a cyclical process of convergence' as opposed to a linear model, which allows for the development of organic communication that embraces both the speaker and the audience.

Audience responsibilities

The excellent tome *Gestures and Acclamations in Ancient Rome* also paints a picture in stark contrast to any linear model of communication. The author, Gregory Aldrete, writes: 'There is no sharp line between performer or communications and the audience for virtually everyone is performing and everyone is listening.'[6]

So, if the audience was participating in the performance in ancient times, what did they do?

ACCLAMATIONS

The first way audiences participated in orations was through their use of 'acclamations', where the members of the audience used their voices and bodies to loudly express pleasure or displeasure, agreement or disagreement, during orations.

In order to allow these displays of real feeling to be expressed publicly and in an authentic way, the social hierarchy had to be, at least to some extent, suspended. A significant Roman virtue was *civilitas*—showing deference to the people and acting as fellow citizens.[7] Adhering to this civilised social code, while still speaking freely, was a vital part of acclamations. Even the emperor was bound by these unspoken rules of etiquette, and it was his job to support the illusion of equality—even when this meant using the herald to ask for silence—so that they did not appear dominant.

Today, as an audience, we may simply clap our hands and supply the odd interjection. However, the system in ancient Rome was far more interesting and unabashed. The different styles of applause included bees, roof tiles and bricks:

- **Bees** did not applaud but hummed, using their mouths to create a vibrating sound.

- **Bricks** held their palms flat and rigid (like bricks) as they clapped.

- **Tiles** clapped with hollowed hands (resembling concave roof tiles).

Audience engagement was not ad hoc—to be expressed however an individual listener felt appropriate. Rather, it was rhythmic, determined by social expectations and often enhanced with words. This was such an effective grouping of techniques that it is said that Nero—after hearing the rhythmic applause of some sailors from a fleet that had just put in—employed 5000 Alexandrians to learn it and use it liberally whenever he sang.[8]

Of course, words were also used. Words could be individual, such as 'feliciter' (good luck), or used to create brief phrases in rhythmic sentences, such as 'So great. So revered. May the gods save you' or

'Rome is safe. Our country is safe, for Germanicus is safe.' Longer chants or even sung phrases might also be employed to demonstrate the audience's approval, agreement or disagreement to what was being said and even the speaker themselves.

The audience might respond using phrases such as: 'Long life to the emperor.' The purpose of this audience–speaker engagement was to constantly define and renew the relationship in the moment and at a fast pace. It must have been exciting, with no individual left pondering their own response in silence. It was active. It was participative. It was noisy.

Through the acclamations alone we can see that this was no linear, one-way engagement: this was a two-way communication. And it was so much part of the ancient Roman way of communication that with his last words, Augustus, like an ageing actor, requested one final acclamation from his audience, saying: 'Have I played the part well? Then applaud me as I exit.'[9]

A CLAQUE

I first learned about the term 'claque' while singing opera in Europe. At the Vienna State Opera, some key soloists would give away tickets to chosen audience members in exchange for immediate and loud applause at the right time—normally at the end of their aria.

The general public would not recognise what was happening, but as professionals we knew when the applause initiated early and carried on longer than was typical. It was (and still is) a very exciting element of the theatres of Europe.

This is also how a claque was used in ancient times, which is where this element of audience participation originated.

Anciently, a claque could initiate applause or lengthen the duration of the applause. But the key job of a claque was to create an enthusiastic display of support, which appeared completely spontaneous. Claque leaders were considered skilled performers — it is said that Heraclius went to bargain with the Avars king not with an army, but with his claqueurs!

Trump uses a claque in a similar way; it is naïve to think that the shouting, cheering and clapping of support and agreement that occurs upon his arrival at an event is always spontaneous. During his presidential campaign, his entrances were always stage managed. Usually, his entrance was preceded by a very loud voice claiming, 'Ladies and gentlemen. Please welcome the next President of the United States', before the chants of 'USA! USA! USA!' began, paced to a deep, slow beat.

This form of audience participation seems new and unusual in our contemporary Western world, but it was a very well-known aspect of communication in the ancient world. It is hugely powerful — a power comes from the real engagement underlying this form of two-way communication, which embraces the audience wholly and completely.

How We See Communication Today

One of my clients sent me a video to review. After watching 30 seconds, I found my focus dwindling and my attention drifting. Basically, I couldn't bear to listen any more. The delivery was static, monotone and delivered with very little thought to the audience (me!). I'm sure I don't need to say more. We've all been there and reached for our smartphones in an attempt to stimulate the mind as a distraction from the speaker.

When I questioned my client on his method of delivery, he said, 'We are conservative.' 'You are boring,' I thought. And in reality, it was worse than boring. It was almost criminal.

The main reason for my criticism of the video was because of the shocking impact on the audience. The speaker is beginning with a mindset that doesn't consider or involve anyone other than themselves. This is typical of many of the real-life engagements that we experience today in that we require no action from the listener. Because of this, we've created a monster (the audience) of whom we ask no action and seek no commitment and from whom we are disconnected and disassociated. And this starts with our modern models of communication.

Modern models of communication

Just as we had Aristotle's Model of Communication, we have modern models as well. But our modern models of communication aren't doing us any favours in terms of learning to communicate with gravitas.

One of these is the communication model of mathematicians Claude Shannon and Warren Weaver, who, in the late 1940s, like those interpreting Aristotle's model, described communication as a linear process. In the Shannon–Weaver Model, the message travels from the 'encoder' or 'sender' to the 'decoder' or 'receiver' along a direct one-way route.[10]

We also have communications expert David Berlo's SMCR Model of Communication (1960), which represents the process of communication in its simplest form, using the acronym SMCR (which stands for sender, message, channel and receiver).[11] In this model, communication is simply the transfer of information from one person to another. So the speaker or sender turns a thought into a message (or encodes the message) and then gives that to the receiver who, in turn, 'decodes' it or turns the message into a thought.

Both of these modern models show a linear path that begins with the sender, or speaker, and ultimately ends with the receiver, or the audience. Researchers began to view communication in this way in the second half of the 20th century and such models seem to always encompass the one-directional arrow that moves from the sender to the receiver.

In other modern models where communication may appear to be two-way at first glance, it soon becomes clear that the direction that the message is travelling continues to go one way only: from the sender to the receiver, with a new interpretation and message going back from the receiver to the sender in a cyclical manner. So while it is travelling between the speaker and their audience, it's still a one-way communication.

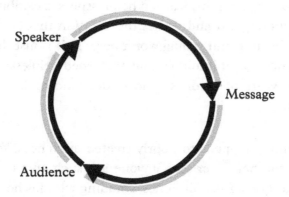

This modern, one-way model of communication simply isn't working, however. And it's led to audiences having two problems: learned helplessness and anxiety.

LEARNED HELPLESSNESS

One of my hobbies is working with two 17.1 hands high (that's big!) warmblood horses called Sir James and Two Stroke. (Why, I hear you ask—as everyone does—the name Two Stroke? It's because when he was born he could not breathe properly and sounded like a two-stroke engine.)

Sir James is smart as a whip, but due to some rather ugly high-level dressage training (before he came to me), he was hit repetitively. And because of that, I have been introduced to the concept of 'learned helplessness'.

Learned helplessness is a state that happens to someone after they have endured a stressful situation or experience repeatedly that is beyond their control. The individual begins to accept that they are powerless, so they simply stop trying to control or change the situation, even when there are opportunities to do so.[12]

For poor old Sir James, his learned helplessness is exhibited when he gets in the round yard and makes the decision that he'd rather just stand there. Hitting and yelling won't help. This is just the treatment that caused him to get into this state of learned helplessness. Instead, it has taken years of kindness and understanding for me to bring him around.

The same thing happens to poorly treated audiences. You will have seen this if you have ever seen anyone ask such an audience if they have any questions. Like Sir James, standing with his head down and disconnected from any provided instruction, the silence is deafening.

Recently, the chair of an organisation exclaimed to me, over and over again, that he never gets any questions from members in his meetings, which he told me emphatically was a clear sign of their agreement. 'Danger! Danger!' I hear the robot from the 1960s TV series *Lost in Space* reiterate. They aren't in agreement, I told him; they simply aren't connecting any more after years of being rebuffed.

In presentations and meetings, learned helplessness applies when participants have become so bored and disengaged that they completely switch off. This is not a simple disconnection, but a severe psychological disengagement as the group members move into survival mode. When this happens, meetings become a kind of dull mandatory activity with no outcome. I see it everywhere. And I see presenters standing behind a lectern with their heads buried in a piece of paper as they speak in an inaudible monotone, their eyes never lifting to those around them.

Another way of looking at learned helplessness is to think of it as a form of cultural autism, with a key characteristic of autism being the difficulty, or impossibility, of developing a 'theory of other'.[13] In the same way that someone on the autism spectrum may struggle to connect with others in a way that lets them really communicate together, your audience's learned helplessness sees them unable to connect with you on the level that lets them buy into and embrace your message—no matter what it is. They simply don't have the capacity to be 'aware' of you as a speaker.

As part of my work, I analyse public figures in the media and speak about communication. Why do journalists want to interview me on the body language of kings, princesses and politicians? Well there is the insight, of course, but also the thrill that the information I share appears to be a completely different perspective from the norm and is a shock to many. We are often just not aware of what is actually going on around these high-profile figures, which indicates how far we are from true awareness of each other.

This inability to build awareness has two repercussions:

- The messages we need to send are not getting through.

- Without awareness, we become incredibly vulnerable to those, perhaps with evil intention, who have a surface gravitas we cannot see through.

Whichever way you put it, we have a problem with communication all round for those being heard (the speaker) and also for those listening (the audience).

ANXIETY

The second issue with the one-way model of communication is the increasing spiral of anxiety. Today's issue is the current increase in numbers of people experiencing anxiety and the consequent silence about the condition, as well as a lack of leaders in so many fields, from health to neighbourhood watch to politics.

It has often been written that the history of anxiety disorders is recent. In fact, many claim that it was hardly known as an illness before the 19th century.[14] But anxiety, as it turns out, is not just a modern phenomenon that only affects 'spoiled millennials'; it is actually a millennia-old condition.[15]

There are indications that anxiety was clearly identified as a distinct and separate disorder by Greco-Roman philosophers and physicians. In addition, ancient philosophy suggested treatments for anxiety that are not too far removed from today's cognitive approaches.[16] Yet, when it comes to performance, oration and singing, we don't see the same impacts anciently as we do today.

Our inability to communicate well in today's world—whether as a leader, an emerging leader or simply in our workplace generally—has led to anxiety; in particular, performance anxiety.

Performance anxiety—sometimes known as 'stage fright' among those who literally take to the stage—is a problem that many people have experienced. This is simply the dread of getting up in front of a group of people and delivering—whether that's a presentation or a performance.

Performance anxiety can be quite serious, and it has impacted many of my clients. If you have performance anxiety, you may experience one or all of these physical symptoms:[17]

- a racing pulse/pounding heart

- rapid breathing

- a dry mouth

- a tight throat

- trembling of the body (hands, knees, lips) and voice

- sweaty and cold hands

- nausea and an uneasy feeling (like 'butterflies') in your stomach

- changes to your vision.

When you experience performance anxiety, it makes it difficult to act at your best. It can impact your ability to communicate, to stay on message and certainly to engage with your audience. This can negatively affect your career, your life, your self-esteem and your self-confidence—all of which will impact your gravitas.

To begin our understanding of this anxiety that many people feel when faced with public speaking, I'd like to introduce two concepts: neural hijacking and alexithymia.

Neural hijacking — when the emotional overrides the rational

When the rational and emotional parts of the brain become desynchronised, this is known as 'neural hijacking' or 'amygdala hijacking'—a theory set out by psychologist Daniel Goleman in his book *Emotional Intelligence*.[18] In essence, the central limbic system (a set of brain structures that help regulate our behavioural and emotional responses) proclaims an emergency and recruits the rest of the brain to deal with that emergency. This is done before the neocortex (our thinking brain) can really understand the situation or take appropriate action. The hallmark of such a hijack is that, once the moment passes, those possessed have the sense of not knowing what came over them.

Goleman gives an excellent example of neutral hijacking in his book. He describes a parent who has been working overtime for more than three weeks. They're already under chronic stress, which has also led to feelings of hopelessness and a loss of control. On top of that they receive a call from their son's school asking them to come in for a meeting to discuss the fact that he's failing. Suddenly their emotional brain takes over, releasing an emotional response that is completely out of proportion to the circumstances.

Something similar happens with the one-way linear model of communication. When the focus is fully on the speaker, neural hijacking leads the speaker to focus on their own issues—questioning their knowledge, their likability and their ability to get their message across to others via this one-way journey. Their emotional mind overwhelms their logical mind and they simply can't focus on their audience, or their message. In other words, it leads to performance anxiety.

This has led to many trainers saying that the key to overcoming performance anxiety is to focus the mind away from ourselves while performing. But once neural hijacking is in full swing, it is hard to reverse. When we experience neural hijacking, we move from rational thought to being highly influenced by negative insecurities, with the rational mind saying, 'You need to be brilliant at this' and the emotional mind screaming, 'Run!'

What is neural hijacking in practice? You would recognise it if you saw it as it has a terrible impact on the ability to speak well. In fact, when a speaker experiences a neural hijacking, they may feel their body jam up, their voice become tight and stifled, and they may even find they're unable to work at all. This physical response is created when circuits in the brain's emotional centres trigger a flood of hormones that put the body on high alert. While the point of this reaction is to help us better evaluate what response to make, the outcome is certainly not a helpful one when we're giving a speech or presentation.[19]

'Neural hijacking' is a term that I use in my new model of communication because it helps me to understand and work with the effects of traumatic stress on the body and voice. Goleman's concept provides a wonderful framework for recognising and managing the catatonic vocal states that I see in some of my clients.

Alexithymia – when rational overrides emotional

Alexithymia—which literally means 'no words for mood'—also impacts our ability to 'perform' while speaking. It is a form of mental malfunction coined by Harvard psychiatrist Peter Sifneos in 1972.[20] The term is used for people who do 'feel', they just don't know they feel and are especially unable to put those feelings into words. They remain passive to the blockage of emotion under minor stress—so they aren't able to recognise or act on their feelings of anxiety or sadness when they have negative or stressful experiences—which then causes *effective blindness* (or 'emotional blindness').[21] This type of effective blindness could otherwise only be surgically imposed by a frontal lobotomy.

Goleman tells us that alexithymia can occur when an incident doesn't incite panic, so the brain's strong functional and logical thought process overrides an emotional reaction. This, in turns, leads to what Goleman describes as 'a grey neutrality'—or a deadened approach—that comes from the inactivity of the prefrontal lobe.

When speakers downgrade—or even suppress—their emotions, they can experience a non-surgical lobotomy (alexithymia), and this can have a serious impact on their ability to speak and communicate well.

Interestingly, as the brain region responsible for working memory, the removal of this part of the brain, known as the prefrontal lobotomy, was thought to be a surgical 'cure' for mental illness in the 1940s because its removal dampened all but the strongest surges of emotion. So, when we suffer from alexithymia, we're also struggling to communicate because our emotions are dulled.

You will recognise the impact of alexithymia in yourself and in others when you see someone speaking with a frozen body and a monotone speech pattern. They'll also demonstrate a lack of inflection, little pitch variation and will even mumble.

So, as an alternative to the panic state of neural hijacking, the person becomes deadened as another way of psychologically 'saving their life'. This essentially becomes their defence mechanism against their fear of public speaking.

'Alexithymia' is another term I use in my new model of communication to signify the effect of chronic stress on the body and voice.

A New Model of Communication: Reshaping the Model for Achieving Gravitas

Research into the ancients' two-way communication, my experience on the stage, working with voice and body, and my practice working with clients who are struggling to communicate well because of anxiety, along with the deadening of audiences who sit in silence, has led me to propose a new model of communication.

This new model is not one that may be useful for telephone wires or any other technical engagement. It is a model specifically for humans in engagement with each other. In this new model, the minute we draw breath together we are one.

It sounds simple but it is important, because the repercussions of getting it wrong are profound. Audiences are dulled, the voice of society is silenced and personally we are left struggling to express ourselves to others.

This new model of communication is a two-way, united model that focuses on plugging the gaps between what the ancients knew, and what we are currently experiencing in the modern world of communication. This means embracing voice (breath) and delivery, with the aim of overcoming our challenges (such as performance anxiety) and thereby increasing our gravitas.

And you may be surprised to know that while this thinking follows the philosophies of the ancient Greeks and Romans, it has an even longer history in ancient cultures, which I would like you to explore further.

Breath as the glue that joins us

In reshaping a model of communication for the modern world—particularly in light of gravitas—I want to reconsider the concept of a non-linear model and turn our thinking to something all inclusive—breath.

From my experience as a singer, I know that the voice moves people. It touches those around you, making people vibrate with your sound. When you breathe in the air of people around you, then the notion of a linear flow of communication simply does not exist—at least not in reality.

I recall the day that I found myself being driven in a taxi by a lovely Fijian man. I asked him, 'How do you say hello in Fijian?' And he said, 'Bhula.' I said, 'Oh, bulla.' And he replied, 'No, it's not buuuuuul-a. It's "boo-la".' As he spoke, he released a huge blast of air behind each word. The breath becomes part of the greeting.

Listening to greetings of ancient cultures, you can hear this again and again. We hear Hawaiians say, 'Alohaaaa' with a huge flow of breath, while the traditional Māori greeting, the hongi, involves pressing noses and foreheads together and sharing air (something many do not realise).

In the article, 'Smell you later',[22] cognitive scientist Kensy Cooperrider writes of the experiences early travellers had with Māori populations and the hongi:

> '[N]ose-forward' greetings … have been observed in the Arctic, Madagascar, New Guinea, Polynesia, and elsewhere. And while they are often described in the subtly sanitized language of 'nose-rubbing,' or as a form of 'kissing,' many of the more detailed descriptions — including Darwin's — suggest that mutual sniffing was a key part.

Inuits share breath as well. Writer, artist and spoken-word poet Taqralik Partridge says: 'We place our nose over the place we intend to kunik [kunik being the Inuit word for the action itself], press our nostrils against the skin, and breathe in, causing the loved one's skin or hair or any other part to be suctioned against our nose and upper lip.'[23]

And think of shalom! An ancient greeting that is delivered with a wonderful puff of air.

Then we move to other species. Animals, just like people, share air as a form of greeting. You breathe me and I breathe you. My work with my horses Sir James and Two Stroke, through natural horsemanship, has shown me so much and I am not alone. Many worldwide are encompassing this work in their leadership programmes. Risking that Two Stroke may well bite your head off if you annoy him, it is important for me to greet him with breath, and I practise the same skills with my animals as we all should with humans. Our breath is the glue that binds us.

This is not quite so animalistic as you might think. Simply by opening your mouth and speaking with others in a greeting, you are exchanging your breath. My point here is not to do anything unusual, but to be aware of that engagement.

This knowledge of the breath as a way we connect is also depicted in our language. As it turns out, the word 'inspire' has an etymology stemming from an association with breath. From the verb 'spirare' (to breathe), the word inspire literally means the act of getting air out of one's own body and into that of the people around you. To 'breathe' air into another is to 'in-spire'.

And we extend the breath to voice. Of course, as humans communicating with each other, unlike with horses, we do not stand and breathe on each other. Instead, we use our voices. It is important to realise that our voice is simply breath broken into air puffs by the cutting movement of the vocal folds. The minute you speak, you share the breath. It's the force of air flow that enters the bodies around you.

In the 19th century, Europeans may have found such practices uncomfortably visceral. They would have been too 'primitive' for their sensibilities, but today it better suits our needs to consider communication as simply the combination of air between two or more people, who by breathing and speaking become one. My new model for gravitas communication will embrace this sharing of air between people and the reawakening of a reference to the flow of air, as this is the vehicle by which sound is made.

A word of warning

The inevitable question arises: what of our modern digital forms of communication?

During the COVID-19 pandemic, we had no choice but to communicate digitally. Following the abatement of the virus it seemed easy to adopt this medium, and the whole 'work from home' discussion that ensued.

But the question we now need to explore is how these digital forms of communication are heightening or diminishing our experience with communication.

As I write, I am speaking worldwide and, along with many others, I find a return to face-to-face conferences and meetings a blessing. Without knowing why, many people found that there was something missing when they were limited to communicating digitally and are finding it to be an enormous relief to engage with people in a group once again.

It is the opinion of many people immersed in communication that our digital media lacks something that is needed to bring us together. We usually turn to the lack of visual presence, but I put it to you that the lack of sharing of breath, which is impossible through a screen, although currently unresearched, will prove to be a stumbling block. Watch this space.

Summary

And so, it seems, we return to the wisdom of the ancients.

Forever, humans have been aware of the breath as an essential part of connection, which we call communication. Our language evolved recognising these principles, and the ancient Romans and Greeks worked with the solid notion of two-way communication, with voices being heard in a continuous flow.

In the 500 years of the Roman Empire, communication was turned into an art form and the Romans moulded the effectiveness of group engagement into a sophisticated interaction. Critical within that was the notion of a two-way exchange. Although the speaker held responsibility for the management of the communication, the speaker and their audience were held in equal regard—and those who managed this effectively had gravitas.

Then, most notoriously in the 20th century, we thought we would get smart and define new models that left these principles to one side.

In Chapter 1, we saw that in today's world we have been ignoring 'delivery' as a critical canon; now, in this chapter, we have seen how Aristotle's model has been depicted as a one-way stream, making our own engagements become boring and disconnected.

As a consequence, audiences have developed 'learned helplessness' and speakers have either developed performance anxiety (neural hijacking) or become deadened (alexithymia) to the world.

Add to our demise a reliance on the virtual media—where breath is no longer shared—and you see our challenge.

To move forward, it is important that we consider how to:

- Connect ourselves again and take action to focus on the audience (large or small) as having equal importance when we speak.

- Be aware that audiences may be suffering from learned helplessness and will need special encouragement.

- Understand neural hijacking and alexithymia when we experience or see it.

- Work with breath as the glue of communication to get it out of our own bodies and make sure that breath is happening actively in others around us.

- Know that our voice is our breath in action, and learn how to get our voice to carry.

- Be aware that engaging 'live' may be the winning KPI (key performance indicator) for the future.

Chapter 3

The Language of the Body

Aldrete notes that, 'A Roman spoke with two languages: verbal and nonverbal.'[1].

As a girl, I was required to deliver a presentation in the school hall. To calm my nerves, my teacher instructed me to stand stock still and simply stare at the clock at the back of the room. Over the years, when I continued to face nerves when performing, I was variously told to imagine that I was in a glass box or that the audience was in the nude.

If you've ever been faced with a case of the nerves (stage fright, or performance anxiety) before delivering a presentation or speaking in front of a group, you probably have heard the same well-meaning but decidedly unhelpful advice. Perhaps these strategies helped you to 'get through' the presentation, but these types of anecdotes certainly won't have helped you to develop that ineffable quality of gravitas that allows you to build engagement and trust with the people around you.

The reason this advice doesn't work is because it's from an age of disassociation: a time when 'survival' (or getting through it) was the only goal. Disassociation is an art form; it is *not* communication. To truly communicate well, we have to have body intelligence—the ability to notice, listen to and respond to body sensations.

Body intelligence is a field that is looking for the true resonance of the body, and the things that stop us from achieving this resonance. For example, I have a beautiful crystal bowl that makes a lovely sound when you run a finger around the edge. Continuing to move the finger around the bowl magnifies that sound and makes it ring magnificently. But if you have your hand flat on the bowl, this blocks the bowl's resonance.

But what does this have to do with communication and gravitas? The ancient Romans and Greeks did not reserve a space for the body in the canons of rhetoric (refer to Chapter 1) because their understanding of the body was integral to their lives. As people still actively involved in combat, they were well aware of the power of the body as an instrument before they ever thought of communicating. Once they were communicating, they recognised the body as an instrument being played to produce the voice and, therefore, their mention of body is incorporated into the canon of 'delivery'.

This book introduces a new model of communication, one that accepts the notion that we are all a set of habitual patterns as opposed to needing 'a natural skill set' or 'having a good voice'. The model focuses on three major areas of new skills—the body, gestures and voice—which will help us to, ultimately, achieve our goal of learning gravitas, and which are covered in this chapter (body), Chapter 4 (gestures) and Chapter 5 (voice).

Body work—working with posture and stance and breath—allows you to embrace body intelligence. And when you can do that you can confidently deliver engaging communications to your audience, helping you to overcome the typical disassociation of delivery and performance anxiety.

This chapter provides very practical steps on how to embrace body work to build your gravitas. But to get there, we need to understand the underpinnings of body work as established by the ancient Romans and Greeks, review where we are currently in our body work and see how the change model can get us to where we need to be to learn gravitas.

The Body in Ancient Greece and Rome

Body work (often referred to as 'sermo corpus' or 'body language') played a vital part in the study of oration in ancient times. It describes the use of the body as an instrument one learned to play during orations (or in our case, communication).

Quintilian explains:

> *All attempts at exciting the feelings must prove ineffectual unless they are enlivened by the voice of the speaker, by his look, and by the action of almost his whole body. For when we have displayed energy in all these respects, we may think ourselves happy if the judge catches a single spark of our fire, and we surely cannot hope to move him if we are languid and supine, or expect that he will not slumber if we yawn.*[2]

Quintilian speaks of body and voice as being inextricably linked, one united instrument; both of these are required to satisfy suitable 'delivery', the most important canon of rhetoric. In fact, Cicero refers to voice and motion as the two constituent parts of action, further cementing the notion that body and voice are integral parts of a whole.

This is a communication ideal that I am a passionate proponent of, having completed a PhD on the connection of the mind, body and voice in line with this ancient thinking—which I call 'vocal intelligence'. However, because of our contemporary notion of body and voice as being separate, I have treated the body and voice separately in this book to allow for their future development by modern speakers today.

So what did the Romans do to bring gravitas to their delivery through body work? Much of the writing on these issues has been lost to time, and there is very little to read about the areas of body work, gestures (Chapter 4) and voice (Chapter 5). But there are, however, some clear areas of body work from where we can glean insights from the ancients' perspective that can guide our own development of gravitas. These are:

1. breath

2. posture

3. gestures of the body.

Breath

Quintilian had a lot to say about breath, knowing that body was breath and breath was sound, and maintaining the breath was a cornerstone of his work.

When it comes to *how* to breathe throughout your orations, there is no further explanation required. Quintilian says it all:

The breathing should be neither short, nor unsustained, nor difficult to recover. The breath, also, must not be drawn too frequently so as to break our sentences to pieces, nor must it be prolonged until it is spent, for the sound of the voice, when the breath is just lost, is disagreeable. The breathing of the speaker is like that of a man held long under water, and the recovery of the breath is long and unseasonable, as being made, not when we please, but when it is compulsory. When we are about to pronounce a long period, therefore, we must collect our breath, but in such a way as not to take much time about it, or to do it with a noise, or to render it at all observable; in other parts, the breath may be freely drawn between the divisions of the matter. [3]

But we ought to exercise the breath so that it may hold out as long as possible. Demosthenes, in order to strengthen his, used to repeat as many verses of a poem as he could in succession while climbing up a hill. And he was accustomed, when he spoke at home, to roll pebbles under his tongue so that he might pronounce his words more freely when his mouth was unencumbered.

Quintilian also describes a failure in the breath as being able to be held for a long time, but which, as a result, becomes tremulous. This shaking voice leads the audience to believe that though the speaker may be strong in appearance, they must nevertheless be weak in the nerves. [4]

Quintilian warns against speakers who suck their breath in through their teeth with a hissing sound, and still others who seem to incessantly pant while they speak, a sound that resembles 'beasts labouring under burdens or in the yoke'. He says that others have a 'tightness of the mouth' which gives listeners the impression that they have to force their words out. 'Coughing, making frequent expectorations, hoisting up phlegm from the bottom of the chest as it were with a windlass, sprinkling bystanders with moisture from the mouth, and emitting the greater part of the breath through the nostrils while speaking', all of these are deemed to be intolerable speaking styles, and disagreeable as well.

Finally, Quintilian advises us how to break up our sentences with our breath, saying that it mustn't be so frequently that it awkwardly parses the sentence into pieces, but it also can't be so prolonged that the breath is lost or the sound of the voice faded.[5]

In summary, we learn from ancient Rome that our breath must be:

1. managed

2. free-flowing

3. drawn during natural breaks in speech

4. supportive of our voice.

Posture

Posture was an important part of gravitas—particularly in presenting yourself to the world—in ancient Rome. Ask yourself, have you ever seen a statue of a Roman emperor with poor posture? The Romans worked their bodies as instruments—they knew that to have real power, it was necessary to be well positioned.

Romans embraced the ideals of fighting men (which makes sense, as many Romans were involved in battle). This body focus carried from the battlefield into the everyday Roman life, and they understood the importance of preparing their bodies through strict attention to correct posture and breath so they could maximise their cardiovascular function. This awareness of the body is evident in the writings of Cicero and Quintilian.

Cicero is summarised as saying: '[The speaker] must practice an economy of movement, with no extraneous effort—the carriage of his body straight and lofty; his pacing measured and kept within bounds; lunging only to the point, and rarely; without effeminacy in turning his head ... '[6]

When you look at statuary from the era of the Roman empire, you'll see the famous 'adlocutio' pose.

This pose—with an arm extended, a finger pointing and the left leg bent—is famed for embodying control, power and leadership. This stance also incorporates the contrapposto pose—a standing position whereby most of the figure's weight is on one leg.

In such statues of emperors, the weight was on one leg for two reasons:

1. to give the body shape

2. to depict movement forward.

While the contrapposto stance depicts a person alone, when another person becomes involved and conversation begins a different position is required. When standing to listen, Quintilian explains,

As to the attitude, it should be erect, the feet a little apart, in similar positions, or the left a slight degree in advance; the knees straight, but not so as to seem stiff; the shoulders kept down; the countenance grave, not anxious, or stolid, or languid; the arms at a moderate distance from the side.[7]

Having a relaxed but confident position of neutrality is important to setting the tone for all your communications, and for ensuring that you feel ready to engage with your audience and communicate with gravitas.

Another element of importance was to have the body in balance. As Cicero notes, 'frequent and rapid oscillation, also, from one side to the other, is objectionable, a habit at which Julius laughed in Curio the father, by asking who it was that was speaking in the boat.'[8] This was a frequent jest, in fact. Another Roman, Sicinius, a leading plebeian (or 'commoner') of the time, made a similar joke, saying that it was only Curio's 'violent tossing about' that saved his sick friend sitting nearby from being devoured by flies.[9]

Quintilian also felt it was vital to keep the head balanced on the body. This might sound obvious, but so many today jam the head into the neck or throw the head forward for power, which is distracting and strangles the throat.

Quintilian observed:

What contributes to gracefulness is, first of all, that the head is held in a proper and natural position, for by casting down the head, humility is signified; by throwing it back, haughtiness; by leaning it on one

side, languor; and by keeping it rigid and unmoved, a certain degree of rudeness.

The neck ought to be straight, not stiff or thrown back. The throat cannot be drawn down or stretched up without equal ungracefulness, though of different kinds, but uneasiness is attendant on the tension of it, and the voice is weakened and exhausted by it. To sink the chin on the breast renders the voice less distinct and, as it were, grosser, from the throat being compressed.[10]

In summary, we learn from ancient Rome that our posture must be:

1. balanced, on two feet with the head held centrally

2. erect, without being stretched or taut

3. natural and easy, without strain

4. supportive of our voice and breath.

Gestures of the body

When it comes to posture, body gestures were part of the overall whole. Romans did not approve of gesticulating with the head alone, which they regarded as a theatrical fault. But Cicero did feel that movements of the whole body are of great importance, insomuch that the effect produced by them builds 'a consummate speaker' even more so than hand gestures.

Extraneous movements, however, were not indulged. Even the flow of breath, which keeps the body in at least some form of constant motion, was heavily regulated. Romans were expected to keep the breath low so it didn't raise the shoulders. Demosthenes is said to have corrected in himself by standing, while he spoke, in a narrow kind of pulpit, with a spear hanging down over his shoulder, so that if, in the warmth of speaking, that gesture escaped him, he might be reminded of it by a puncture from the weapon.[11]

From Ancient to Modern

It was in Vienna that I first learned about body intelligence and body work as it pertained to voice and performance. I discovered the work of German-Austrian fencer Professor Ellen Müller-Preis, a renowned expert in the subject who worked from the early 1950s with singers and actors at the Vienna State Opera, the Burgtheater, the Frankfurt University of Music and Performing Arts, and Salzburg Festivals, and who would become my mentor for 12 years until her death. I aided her in masterclasses in Vienna, Salzburg, Linz, Cardiff, London, Sydney and Brisbane.

Professor Müller-Preis didn't only work with performers. She also studied medicine and competed (and won medals) in fencing at five Olympic Games. From her personal experiences, she formed a theory that voice training should always be preceded by integrated body training, which would allow the body to breathe. She says about breath work, 'if you let the body breathe, then you let the body sing'.[12]

In retrospect, I recognise this world of opera was brimming with the legacy of ancient Rome and offered possibly the closest connection one could make to the discipline and practice of the orators 2000 years previous.

I found that the things that worked well aligned with something different, something I now recognise as the perspectives of the ancients. Over time I have realised it was a long way from the work and the perceptions that had developed in Western culture over the past century. We are being led astray, and this is impacting our ability to use our bodies to deliver our communications, and undermining any ability to present with gravitas.

Contemporary body work

In the last 70 years, the fields of study on body and communication have been divided into disparate fields in an attempt to analyse and bring clarity to how we might improve.

In 1952, anthropologist Ray Birdwhistell[13] wanted to study how people communicate through their bodies. You cannot help but be captivated by his studies, which show 'the average person actually speaks words for a total of about 10 or 11 minutes a day and that the average sentence takes only about 2.5 seconds. Birdwhistell also estimated we can make and recognise around 250 000 facial expressions.'[14]

Birdwhistell estimated that the verbal component of a face-to-face conversation is less than 35 per cent while over 65 per cent of communication is nonverbal. Albert Mehrabian, a pioneering researcher of body language in the 1950s, is attributed to saying that the total impact of a message is about 7 per cent verbal (words only), 38 per cent vocal (including tone of voice, inflection and other sounds) and 55 per cent nonverbal.[15]

Other researchers, such as Paul Ekman,[16] have added extensively to the research of nonverbal communication with regard to facial expressions, hand and arm gestures, postures, positions and various movements of the legs and feet, but in the end we are drawn to one focus—body language—and how it impacts our perception of others.

There are some in our time who have done astounding work around body language. One is Arthur Lessac, expert in voice-speech, renowned Broadway vocal coach and the developer of Lessac Kinesensic Training. Arthur Lessac wrote the book *Body Wisdom: The Use and Training of the Human Body*, and in it he introduces the term 'body intelligence'.[17] This work was mostly recognised in the acting profession, but though Lessac trained as a singer in America he soon developed an interest in the human body in general and focused his work on body kinesiology (the study of movement).

Lessac's work is based on the idea that the speaker must 'eliminate all anaesthetic, deadening habits in his or her communicative behaviour and replace them with an ongoing state of habitual awareness'.[18] Lessac believed that 'voice and speech training is body training and body training is language/communication training, as well as bio-neuro-psychic heightened sensitivity training'.[19]

Body work in voice builds on much earlier work, including that of Matthias Alexander, an actor suffering constant vocal loss, which he traced to body misalignment. As a result, Alexander developed techniques of postural alignment (known as the Alexander technique) that have become synonymous with postural excellence as a basis for good health.

Sadly, Alexander's work was never recognised during his lifetime. While his work is now beginning to infiltrate classical singing training in Australia, while he was alive he was 'up against it to convince the scientific world that the methods were sound; particularly as he has no scientific language but only the ways of the ordinary world'.[20]

Lessac and others like him are outliers in what 'modern experts' consider important for us all to know when communicating. So while there are some doing marvellous work, it has not permeated the mind of the modern communicator and instead we have moved our focus elsewhere.

Our modern fascination with body language

As early as 1889, Cesare Lombroso, an Italian criminologist anxious to make a connection between physical anomalies and criminal tendencies, published his book *L'Uomo delinquente*. It was not until nearly 30 years later that nonverbal studies began to take shape in earnest, with German psychiatrist Ernst Kretschmer's book, *Physique and Character*,[21] followed in 1940 by American psychologist WH Sheldon's *The Varieties of Human Physique*[22] and anthropologist David Efron's *Gesture and Environment* in 1941.[23] These works were based on the idea that, if we precisely measure and analyse a person's body, we can learn much about his or her intelligence, temperament, moral worth and future achievement. (Given the issues of the war and ethnic cleansing in Europe during the time of these studies, these works were highly provocative. In fact, Sheldon's personal notes have revealed him as drawing racial conclusions from his work. In 1951, he featured on the cover of the popular magazine *Life*, but he was unable to prove the validity of his perceptions, nor have any researchers since.)

We know today that the direction these authors took was false and was soon replaced by ideas around 'body language', including those explored in Australian body language expert Allan Pease's book *The Definitive Book Of Body Language*,[24] which created enormous interest on the corporate speaking circuit. Other body language experts, such as Joe Navarro[25] and Kasia Wezowski,[26] have produced bestsellers that are marvellous reads.

My criticism of the direction we have taken with this work is tainted by the fact that I myself am considered a leading global expert in the field, make regular media appearances analysing public figures and have a fascination with the perception of others. I have received 2.5 million clicks for my analysis of various world events and am intrigued by the interest of others in my version of events through an analysis of the body and voice. I also recognise the failings of viewing a person through this perspective as a single means of analysis, so I am committed to bringing you along with me on a different track towards understanding and learning gravitas.

What I recognise is that body language has dropped the ball in three ways:

1. It denies the co-existence of voice as inextricably linked with the body.

2. It focuses on perception, which, while of interest, should not be the sole focus for anyone who communicates.

3. It disentangles itself from the difficulties of change through understanding and learning gravitas, by laying all bets on a model of 'fake it to make it'.

Somehow, we have become hoodwinked by an understanding of body language that is all glitz and glow but that has actually taken us further from where we need to be as communicators.

WHAT PART DOES PERCEPTION PLAY?

'Nonverbal studies' hold the study of perception as a critical focal point. Modern research on body work relies on the belief that how we are perceived depends less on the real experiences of the listeners, and more on our belief that we 'know how the world works'.

And it is not suggested we ignore perception. It has its place. It is ever present and 'whether or not we can interpret them correctly, whether or not speaker and listener would agree to their significance, these nonverbal but nonetheless primary aspects of the exchange play an important part in the perception of persons'.[27] But this focus on perception, while interesting, should not be the sole focus for anyone who communicates (or even the primary focus). Instead, we should be looking *beyond* perception, which has never been a suitable strategy for change.

You see, by taking body language as the sole focus of what goes on, we move to the assumption that by simply changing what people see or hear, we will solve the problem.

However, that is just not enough to remedy the gap in our communications. For instance, if you realise the perception of your speech is that you speak too fast, you may think you should speak more slowly—wrong. If you are told you continually say 'um', you may think you simply need to stop saying 'um'—but this doesn't work. If others observe you're waving your hands, you may decide you should just stop gesturing—absolutely not!

SHOULD WE JUST 'FAKE IT TO MAKE IT'?

The implication of modern research is that when it comes to body language, the speaker is to 'fake it to make it', a view reflected in a comment I heard one night on the popular television series *Friends*: 'Honesty is the key to a relationship. If you can fake that, you're in.'

For instance, we are told that folding one's arms means that a person is being defensive or closed: 'The message received by the other person is that the person is not entirely comfortable with this conversation and wants to be protected from damage. The gesture generally works against trust because information is perceived to be blocked.'[28]

There is no denying that this may well be the case. However, does this information provide enough of an impetus for change for the average person? The answer I usually hear in my work (and I hear it over and over) is that this position feels comfortable and 'authentic'. The solution to simply stop doing it does not provide enough of an impetus to make change.

Consequently, the usual outcome is we settle for our fascination for analysing the body language of others, but we leave our own change to the wind.

What needs to be explained is that perception of others is only part of the story. It is fascinating to know that others may perceive this as being blocked, but another impetus is that it actually *is* blocked. The arms placed across the body is exactly where the diaphragm (a muscle that helps you breathe in and out) lies under the lungs. The folded arms block the ability to breathe and to then make sound. There is no way this 'sound bowl' of a body can resonate in this position.

After explaining this, I usually see a far greater willingness to change than I would by simply relying on the perception of others as the impetus for change.

As for the authenticity, we mistake poor habitual patterns as 'natural'. Personally, I prefer not to hear the word 'natural' in my workshops as it underlies a person's limiting belief in their ability to change. Often in life, what someone is doing is not natural—it is habitual. Surely something 'authentic' is an action that fits with our values and allows us to perform to our best.

I remember a CEO (who I knew to be genuinely concerned about employee feedback) who beautifully demonstrated how our modern approach to communication and body language has let us down. First, he fumbled for words throughout his presentation, often staring at the floor. And then, once his presentation was over, he aggressively asked for questions. 'What sort of questions would you like, Mr X?' asked one brave engineer. 'Any question you ask will be a career decision' was the insecure and angry reply. It was a lose–lose situation for all concerned.

I noticed that during his presentation he demonstrated significant facial and neck tension and, sometimes, a complete stiffness and lack of any facial movement. His posture included a tightened, slightly hunched upper back and folded arms. From my singing experience, this led me to understand that the ability of the diaphragm to do its work was blocked, leading to an obstructed airflow.

In the absence of an ability to produce vocal tone effectively, the speaker is left with only the options of either sloppy articulation and airless droning or, by putting more pressure on the vocal system, the harsh strength of squeezed-out, hard glottal attacks, tight, nasal vowels and spat consonants.

This posture and vocal articulation was accompanied by putting most of the body weight on one leg, giving the psychological impression of being casual or 'not caring', which was contrary to what I knew was his true intention.

Dropping the ball with breath, posture and body gestures

Our modern teaching and skills around breath, posture and body gestures continues to leave us with far too many skills gaps in our communications.

As we see with the CEO in the preceding section, posture is an important part of your nonverbal communication, and when you do it poorly, you're left communicating the misleading perceptions. When we aren't taught the appropriate skills of stance and posture when delivering, we end up with a crisis of confidence—shifting uneasily on stage, rocking from foot to foot or, worse, adjusting our hair or even genitals while trying to speak.

We can have a similar experience with body gestures. When we aren't taught what to do with our heads and eyes, for example, we end up using our body in a way that leads to miscommunication and confusion in our messaging. When we aren't understood, we lose trust—and we certainly lose gravitas.

And, of course, we're also falling down with breath. In my experience, over decades of workshops, maybe only about 1 per cent of people know where the vocal folds (where the sounds used for speech are produced) exist in the body, and few people can 'pin the tail on the donkey' to find the diaphragm. Eighty per cent of participants are breathing using a stress pattern that comes from a jamming of the diaphragm, and the movement of the stomach goes in the exact opposite direction to that which it should. (I explain this further later in this chapter in the section 'The skills of breath'.)

People who attend yoga and other meditation or breathwork classes are often able to work with their breath in those contexts, but find it challenging to transfer their breathing skills when communicating.

The most common statement I hear is, 'I run out of breath', whereas, as Professor Müller-Preis would say, 'You never run out of breath. You only run into tension.'

Which leads us to my model of change (introduced in Chapter 2).

Learning Gravitas

Whether we are considering the body, the breath, gestures, the voice or any aspect relevant to a new focus on 'delivery', there needs to be a model for change that is simple and actionable.

My change model adopts the following principles:

- Each person is born with a perfect instrument (body and voice).

- All people can express themselves.

- There are no bad sounds, although sometimes there are unhealthy sounds.

- Voice, body and mind are inextricably linked.

As a child, I used to play a game where you had to say an object and the next child had to remember that object and then add a new one. The third child had to say those two objects and add another—and so it went on.

A bit like the child's game of remembering, this new model of communication has a few connected steps it will be helpful to recall. It can be tricky to remember each step, but there are five simple areas to consider and reconsider as you move forward.

These steps (all questions) are as follows:

- What are you doing now?

- What is your impetus for change?

- What do you want to be doing?

- How will you practise the new way?

- What are the barriers to success?

We do this for every single skill and technique we have.

Take the example of standing on one leg and ask these five questions.

1. What are you doing now?

It may be that, when challenged, you drop one knee when you speak.

2. What is your impetus for change?

From a body language perspective, this may seem like you do not care about the issue at hand.

From a reality perspective, it may be a habit originally initiated by a feeling of weakness or being under threat as a child. We drop our energy and drop one leg, perhaps as a reflection of a need to run (fight or flight).

However, when you drop one leg, a consequence is that the pelvic floor is tilted — and thus the pelvic diaphragm is tilted. The diaphragm of the pelvic floor mirrors the movement of the diaphragm under the lungs. These are two completely separate diaphragms, one in the pelvis and the other attached to the bottom of the rib cage and cutting the body in half horizontally (which is the one you have likely heard of before). However, if the movement of one diaphragm is limited, this limits the capability of the other. In other words, standing on one leg means your ability to breathe, and hence speak, is limited.

3. What do you want to be doing?

It's simple. Stand on two legs!

4. How will you practise the new way?

In order to practice staying balanced on two legs when facing confrontation or negativity, I would suggest going into a shop and asking for something they do not sell. For example, walk into a chocolate shop and ask for coffee. When they say, 'we don't make coffee', be conscious to stand on two legs to have balance (and gravitas) and say, 'Oh, sorry. Thank you very much.'

My point here is to challenge yourself in a non-confrontational environment so you can begin to become aware of your patterns. You create a new habit through the practice of using the skills of gravitas every day in every way.

Either that or come to one of my retreats and have me sort it out, but you can do it on your own if you understand and practise the principles of reflection (which I describe in the next section).

5. **What are the barriers to success?**

You may be thinking, 'Oh, that sounds silly,' which is, of course, a major barrier to success. We always feel silly doing something we have not always done. Our major barrier is the desire to stay in the same pattern of doing what we have always done.

Using these five questions will help you move through the learning cycle, from unconscious incompetence to conscious incompetence. As we learn the skills we need to become competent, we move to conscious competence and then attempt the giant leap to unconscious competence, where we have managed to change our communication pattern from what we have always done, to what will work much better for us.

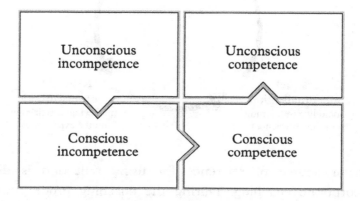

The phrase I use constantly is, 'The amateur practises until they get it right. The professional practises until they can't get it wrong.'

Who first said this is a mystery and it has been repeated by many, but it is the slogan of the professional. And it gives us the answer of how to change, particularly when it comes to body work. And the answer to change is practice, practice, practice.

Practice, practice, practice

One of the myths of practice that I'd like to debunk is that 'practice makes perfect'. It does not. More accurate is 'practice of the right things makes perfect'. Finding the right things requires us to use the practice of reflection—or reviewing the experiences that we had during our practice, and making adjustments as necessary.

Psychologist David Kolb's learning cycle is one practical way to use the critical function of reflection in your own practice.

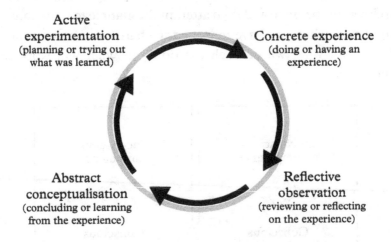

Active experimentation
(planning or trying out what was learned)

Concrete experience
(doing or having an experience)

Abstract conceptualisation
(concluding or learning from the experience)

Reflective observation
(reviewing or reflecting on the experience)

My major source of reference for using reflection is derived from corporate coaching. During the coaching process, we use reflection as 'sense-making'. In other words, it helps us to make the transition from implicit practice, skill and knowledge to the explicit acknowledgement, naming and framing of those things.[29]

WORKING WITH OUR IMPLICIT AND EXPLICIT SKILLS

I have found with my clients, through working with the body and through constant reflection, that they could constructively involve implicit and explicit skills of body work within the spaces of communication and gravitas.

But what are implicit and explicit skills?

- **Implicit skills.** Tacit — or implicit — knowledge is considered 'knowledge that enters into the production of behaviours and/or the constitution of mental states but is not ordinarily accessible to consciousness'.[30]

- **Explicit skills.** Explicit knowledge or skills are those that can be accessed, used and enhanced by the rational/logical brain. In other words, they're easily available for you to use in your communications.

There are four basic patterns for creating knowledge and skills. These are:[31]

1. **From implicit to implicit.** These patterns start with skills or knowledge known through observation, imitation and practice, where little systematic (that is, shareable) insight into craft can easily be leveraged.

2. **From explicit to explicit.** These patterns involve collecting, combining and synthesising many existing pieces of explicit knowledge from different areas of your experience, making it possibly more accessible or more likely to be used.

3. **From implicit to explicit.** These patterns involve the conversion of local knowledge into explicit knowledge that can be accessed, used and enhanced by the rational/logical brain.

4. **From explicit to implicit.** These patterns involve the internalisation of knowledge by others, so that their own 'artistry' — to use philosopher Donald Schön's term — is

broadened, extended and reframed. Experts also refer to this as 'becoming *consciously unknowing* and *consciously unskilled*'.[32]

There is a place for all these processes within our work, incorporating all levels of body work, including posture, body gestures and breath (including voice).

CAPTURING IMPLICIT SKILLS

I want to further explore the possibilities of movement from implicit to explicit. As Michael Polanyi describes,[33] we know more than we can tell and, to help us understand the challenges of capturing these implicit skills, we have to understand that implicit knowledge can be highly personal and hard to formulate.

Implicit knowledge is understanding that is rooted in action. In other words, it's knowledge that's gained because an individual is an expert in a craft or profession, technology or product. These are partly technical skills, like those developed by a master craftsperson after years of experience, but with a mental component. Ikujiro Nonaka, professor emeritus at Hitotsubashi University in Tokyo, describes implicit knowledge in the *Harvard Business Review* as having 'an important cognitive dimension. It consists of mental models, beliefs and perspectives so ingrained that we take them for granted, and therefore cannot easily articulate them.'[34]

A great deal of our day-to-day experience is within our awareness but is implicit in the sense that no verbal or other symbols have been attached to it. This kind of experience is 'felt meaning' (we know it, but we don't know how we know it) and includes in it the inward sense of our body, its tension, its wellbeing. It is essentially a sensory, visceral, intuitive and—sometimes—emotional experience.

Before we really solidify these into practical actions, these 'felt' meanings are tacit, implicit, incomplete, pre-conceptual, waiting for us to 'organise' or 'make sense' of them in many different ways. In the tradition of existential thinking, our feelings are 'possibilities'—possible actions in the world.

When we are looking for ways to transform implicit 'knowingness' into explicit, articulated understanding that we can use in our communications, we can turn to the process of 'reflection-in-action'. This is where we focus on attending and actively listening to our own internal data. Some ways you can undertake reflection-in-action is by journalling, recording your presentations or speeches, or gathering feedback from your colleagues or associates.

REPRESENTING KNOWLEDGE

The question then becomes: what form will that knowledge take? There is no one 'best' way to represent this new knowledge. Each problem requires a unique style of thinking. However, one of the most frequently overlooked tools is the use of metaphor.

Metaphor has always been helpful when 'sense-making'. In this case, by metaphor we do not mean just a grammatical structure or allegorical expression, but rather a distinctive method of perception. It is a way of starting the dialogue about the new skills and knowledge, and establishing a connection between those two things to allow for creative discussion.

Using metaphor to surface choice

One of my clients, Pat, described his voice as a 'rusty Meccano set, which needs RD40 [lubricant]'. I shared my view that his voice was actually a fully functioning machine. However, he sometimes drove with his foot on the accelerator and sometimes with his foot on the brake. Braking and accelerating concurrently, the car (a metaphor for his voice) was leapfrogging along, rather than running smoothly. We investigated these metaphors further and, from a topic that held enormous emotional pain, we found ourselves laughing and discussing the issues in a relaxed and interactive conversation.

The key difference between us was that Pat's metaphor implied there was something rusty or corroded about his voice. However, my feeling was that there was nothing wrong with his voice but rather with the way he was operating it.

Another client, Bob, reminded me of the story of the boy with the red balloon.[35] In this story, the boy is running, looking skywards, dreaming, with a huge red balloon. That was Bob, his emotions held high above him.

We included in this metaphor the feedback from Bob's colleagues that his emotions were detached. It helped us to combine the image of Bob being 'vague and interesting' with his colleagues' seeing him as 'emotionless'. Certainly, the boy with the red balloon looking skywards sees many things, but one of them is not his own body and the people around him.

Practical strategies

Metaphor can help us turn implicit skills into explicit skills, and to embrace this knowledge and capability into our lives. Of course, there are many practical skills that we have developed to conquer the modern challenges posed in body work—namely posture, body gestures and breath. And much of this we can bring into play from our understanding of how it was handled by the ancient Romans and Greeks.

The skills of breath

One of the fascinating and counterintuitive practical strategies we can use to solve the modern challenge of breath is to work on the 'breath out', as opposed to the 'breath in'. In most situations, when people are learning about voice and speaking, the focus is on getting enough breath in. But by focusing on the breath out, we're changing the paradigm altogether.

Firstly, re-focusing on the breath out is embracing the idea of breath as an element of communication (as discussed in Chapter 2). It is the breath out we need for speaking, so we need to consider how we focus on that breath more effectively, rather than putting our focus on the breath in (which will happen automatically as a vacuum recoil so long as we have got enough air out in the first place).

Secondly, when we focus on the breath out rather than the breath in, we're essentially breaking a habitual thought pattern. It is my understanding, through my work with body and singing, that focusing on the breath out is far more likely to break stress patterns (which are often associated with the breath in), making those patterns difficult to alter.

I find my clients are often shocked that the stomach naturally goes in for the breath out, just as it does during laughter and light coughing. They want it to go out, but then I explain that such an action is against the forces of nature and the result of a habitually jammed diaphragm.

So with breath, the change pattern may look as follows:

1. What are you doing now?

A common strategy for many under stress is to 'take in a deep breath to relax'.

When I work with my clients on deep breathing for stress, I will ask them to show me how that works. Usually the person will breathe in and the chest will expand and raise up.

I then suggest we experiment with a breath 'out' to discover what happens. Often as a consequence of the inherent psychological stress, we discover that the stomach actually pops out and the chest depresses.

2. What is your impetus for change?

One needs to realise that the high breath is caused by a stress response that jams the diaphragm under the lungs.

The impetus for change is threefold.

Firstly, when one has this pattern in reverse, when you breathe in, the chest raises and the stomach goes in. This looks tense and stressed to the observer.

Secondly, by raising the chest, the vocal mechanism can become compromised, meaning your larynx will be squeezed.

Thirdly, by breathing this way, the amount of air one actually receives into the lungs is limited and you will struggle to be oxygenated. The brain needs oxygen. You will find you can't think clearly.

3. What do you want to be doing?

Firstly, I point out that the strategy for communication is not about relaxing. It is about being energised to express yourself.

Secondly, the healthy pattern for the breath is to have the stomach going 'in' for a breath out.

4. How will you practise the new way?

Firstly, I recommend that you look at a video of the breath in motion. There are many 3D videos of the lungs and diaphragm in action, and you will see the rationale behind the movement of the stomach in response to the breath in and out.

Then we learn the Kapalbhati breath, another topic to search online as there are many good videos available. This is a yoga breath, which I learned while singing and with which I have had enormous success when coaching people with performance anxiety.

The Kapalbhati breath requires you to bring under control a conscious fast breath out with the stomach going in. This movement is like a kick into the stomach, which in turn pushes up under the diaphragm to release it.

If you have another technique that works for you, please use it. Some people may find they can breathe in and deeply with ease under stress, but most of us, and certainly those with performance anxiety, simply can't do that easily.

Also be aware that it is very easy for the unconscious mind to fool you. For instance, you may tell yourself that the stomach goes 'out' for the breath 'out'. This is not substantiated anywhere and makes no sense, but because it is a habitual pattern you will tell yourself *ad nauseum* that this must be exactly what needs to happen.

5. **What are the barriers to success?**

The unconscious mind is a fascinating thing. It will convince you that your old pattern is correct. You may convince yourself it is 'natural' to do the stress pattern and that you 'have' to do it.

You may tell yourself it is 'too hard' to change or you may feel really (psychologically) comfortable in the old pattern. Recognising what is going on for you is the key, as is being fascinated by the unconscious mind. Personally, I also find it humorous to see the unconscious mind as a little puppet on my left shoulder. I know it is trying to help by giving me defensive responses. So I recognise that and speak with it. I say, 'Well done, but that's not a suitable response right now, so we are going to do what we know is actually a far more effective reaction.'

Summary

The consequence of a lack of strategy for our skills has led us to hide our bodies behind a big wooden block (the lectern) in the weakest part of the stage or room, with a static microphone to project our voices over the most pathetic of distances.

Somewhere along the pathway of communication, we have become far too focused on IQ, on expertise, and we attempt to fulfil the requirements of impactful speechmaking and influential communications by focusing only on words—and not on delivery. And because our modern work on nonverbal communication—such as body work and body intelligence—has been so limited, we're left with only our own self-guidance (an inadequate tool) for improvement.

In my experience, there is little effective communication occurring in boardrooms, conference stages or university lectures. Difficult situations are avoided, feedback is neglected, and we stand behind lecterns placed tragically at the side of the stage, giving away our power to what we aptly call PowerPoint. We have stopped working to develop our quality of voice, our breath work or our posture.

What this results in is modern leaders, emerging leaders and, in fact, all individuals who are looking to communicate with others experiencing repeated failure. And that has brought serious blows to self-esteem, confidence and, ultimately, gravitas.

The key here is to face the challenges head on. Yes, body language as it has developed over the last 30 years is fascinating, but it is not everything and, in particular, it is not a model for change.

The model for change and the practical solutions in this chapter are designed to help us refocus on the vitally important element of body work. As your nonverbal and verbal skills become more aligned, this will help to reinvigorate your confidence, build trust with your audience and then lead to more gravitas in your speaking overall.

Of course, nonverbal skills don't stop here. We also have to focus on the skills of gestures — the focus of the next chapter.

Chapter 4

Gestures

*Though the peoples and nations of the earth speak a multitude
of tongues, they share in common the universal language of
the hands.*

— Quintilian[1]

To the ancients, gestures were as natural a function as
breathing itself. They had meaning, there were rules, they were
marked in written text and they were well understood by all
and sundry. They took up a major proportion of the discussion
on delivery within the five canons of rhetoric (covered in
Chapter 1), sharing the role with voice and body. Delivery was
the most important canon of rhetoric; with gestures holding a
critical role in delivery, their importance is clear.

What went wrong? Why, today, are gestures abhorred? And why do
we have such black and white thinking that has led to many people
being told they over-gesture—the solution for which is to stand with
the hands frozen to the side?

There is a fear around gestures today. Conventional wisdom tells us they are distracting, overwhelming and unprofessional. But research—both ancient and modern—reveals otherwise. And with understanding we can claw back skills clearly outlined by the ancients and revered until the last century, but lost.

In this chapter, we look at the perspectives of the past and present to find ways we can utilise gestures to improve gravitas. Developing these skills will be beneficial for the people around you and help you to build confidence and influence when speaking.

Gestures in Ancient Greece and Rome

Demosthenes was said to have performed his speeches in front of a mirror before delivering them in public so that he could cement his gestures.[2] Roscius (126–62 BCE), a famous Roman comic actor, carefully practised every gesture he planned to make on the stage beforehand in private.[3] Hortensius (114–50 BCE), the renowned Roman lawyer, orator and statesman, was also known to deliver powerful speeches supported by emphatic gestures that were said not to carry the same weight when written.[4] But it was Cicero whose hands were considered so lethal in their influence that they needed to be sliced from his body on his death.

In 43 BCE, Mark Antony (83–30 BCE) ordered the murder of Cicero for using his unparalleled powers of speech to work against Antony. And, as was common for the day, Cicero was beheaded by a group of assassins. But, uncommon for the day, as well as losing his head, Cicero's hands were also severed and placed on the rostra in Rome with his head between them.

Gestures comprise a major part of the pillar of Aristotle's rhetoric known as 'delivery'. Together with voice, gestures played a critical role in oration in ancient times, with orators taught to use their hands, arms and fingers to express more than their words themselves could do on their own.

Why did the ancients focus on gestures?

In ancient times, the most important events were not held in an enclosed space but rather in the open air. This included gladiatorial combats, beast hunts, chariot races and theatrical performances. But it also included funerals, triumphs (military parades), religious ceremonies and festivals, holidays, court trials, voting procedures and political assemblies. Even criminal trials were held in the open air. It was unheard of to choose a stifling internal venue with no reference to the external world. It was as foreign to the ancients as having meetings in a park would be to us today.

Each of these events required the work of powerful orators, announcers of the event, politicians and statesmen arguing points of policy and actors preparing to take to the stage. These individuals were each striving for the greatest impact and the most effective delivery of their message, whatever form it was to take. That meant ensuring the most effective use of gestures.

The Romans understood that an orator spoke with two languages: verbal and nonverbal. And so they focused on these elements—particularly gestures—just as much as the words themselves, and possibly even more.

When it comes to verbal and nonverbal communication—in this case, gestures—the messages that the two languages convey could be identical, complementary or even different. For example, when using gestures, the eyes of the orator would typically follow the movement involved with their gestures. This demonstrated accordance or harmony with the communication. However, if they used a gesture against the movement of the eye, they could be conveying disharmony, condemnation or even aversion to the fact or opinion being communicated.[5] This can be seen in the gesture of aversion—two hands pushing away from the body while the head is turned away—where the head and hands move in different directions.

Gestures, then, extended the listener's deep understanding of the communication, adding emotional colouring. It was a way to achieve eloquence not only with the word but with their entire bodies. In fact, certain gestures were associated with various emotions, so that as an orator spoke, his body could offer a separate, complementary and continuous commentary on what emotions his words were intended to provoke. For example, he could demonstrate grief by clenching his hand to his chest, followed by anger at what had occurred by slapping his hand against his thigh. This would eloquently portray the emotions that accompanied his words.

Inviting emotion into delivery was a significant part of ancient oration. With a lack of emotion, any speech would fall short, losing its audience and therefore its message.

Berating orator Marcus Calidius, Cicero said:

There was no significant agitation, neither in your mind, or in your body. Did you strike your forehead? Did you slap your thigh? Or at the very least stamp your foot? In fact, so far from inflaming my emotion, I nearly fell asleep on the spot.[6]

In ancient times, gestures also served a metronomic function. Like a metronome used in piano classes, the tick, tick, tick of the rhythm would keep orators on track with their orations. Likewise, gestures monitor, coordinate, maintain or control the pace and flow of conversations. Like a conductor with their arms accentuated by a banner, we conduct the music of our conversations with our hands. Like a singer, the hands guide the flow of air. In fact, Quintilian tells us that voice and gestures are inextricably linked and that gestures 'must be in concert with the voice and must, as well as the voice, obey the mind'.[7]

Gesture was such an integral part of the ancients' overtly public life that people became highly attuned to the nonverbal aspects of communication. Emperor Titus Caesar Vespasianus (79–81 BCE) could tell jokes by gesture alone. Artists created sculptures, paintings and other artworks that drew the emperors' hands larger in proportion—demonstrating the focus on the hands for communication.

Powerful orators could include more visual accompaniments, and they could even give prearranged signals to members of the audience. In one famous example, before the assassination of Julius Caesar (100–44 BCE), senator Tillius Cimber grabbed hold of Caesar's toga and pulled it down from his neck, which signalled to the other conspirators that it was time to attack.[8]

In another example, Pompey the Great (106–48 BCE), one of the great statesmen and generals of the Roman Republic, was given the command against pirates in 67 BCE.[9] Roscius was able to express, through gestures alone, the fairly complex message that he opposed the plan and thought one man should not be given so much power. He then proposed an alternate plan where a second commander would be appointed who would share power with Pompey—again, through gestures alone.

The rules

For the system of gestures to function properly, the speaker and audience had to know what the rules were or, at the bare minimum, be conditioned to act in more or less predictable ways. Ideally, there would have been both self-conscious knowledge of the rules and at least a tacit agreement to abide by them.

One rule was that an orator should never use the left hand alone. The main exception was counting with the fingers or adjusting their clothes, though an orator should rarely adjust their clothing during a presentation. Instead, they should always present the character of a man of dignity and virtue, which is, of course, a part of gravitas.

Gestures at the beginning of the oration were considered the most important and given the most thought and weight when the orator was preparing his speech. However, throughout the entire speech orators were trained to use one gesture for every three words (Cicero's percentage was eight gestures for every 17 words). In practice, the gestures and the accompanying verbalised thoughts would begin and end together—inextricably linked.

Even in written speech, outlined as a precursor to presentation, gestures were included and described for the reader to understand. They were placed within brackets (< >) to inform the reader that they were separate from the spoken word.

Finally, in ancient times, it was believed that by the time you had completed your oration with its accompanying gestures, sweat should be pouring from the shoulder and your clothing should be dishevelled. This would demonstrate that you had given your full energy to your delivery or performance for your audience.

Dimensions

The Romans point out that gestures—particularly whole-body gestures—occur in three-dimensional space, just like the world we live in. This means they use all directions, such as in front of the speaker, above, below, to the sides, and so on. They also embrace seven basic movements:

1.   left

2.   right

3.   up

4.   down

5.   forwards

6.   backwards

7.   circular.

These movements are represented in every specific gesture that you will see or use throughout your delivery. (Aristotle did not mention the seventh movement, 'circular', in his list, but it was added later by Quintilian.[10])

Of course, each orator also introduced their own specific interpretation of the gestures and how they used them. We can view the use of gestures like a recipe. Each gesture is an ingredient, and the recipe is set to create a certain message or communication. But as every good chef knows, there is always room for creativity. However, out of necessity, the more formal gestures of ancient Roman orators would remain closely aligned to the widely understood gestures of the common Romans of the time so that their message could be accurately and effectively conveyed to their audience.

Some of the gestures depicted in the documents, vases and murals are captured in Aldrete's work.[11] Overleaf are some depictions.

Mistreatment and ill-fortune*

Humility**

Overhearing a secret***

Emphasis****

*Miniature for act 3, scene 3, lines 361—414, from the illustrated manuscript of the Hecyra of Terence, Vat. Lat. 3868, folio 70r

**Miniature for act 4, scene 4, lines 610—35, from the illustrated manuscript of the Adelphi of Terence, Vat. Lat. 3868, folio 59

***Miniature for act 4, scene 2, lines 577—606, from the illustrated manuscript of the Hecyra of Terence, Vat. Lat. 3868, folio 72v

****Miniature for act 4, scene 1, lines 567—90, from the illustrated manuscript of the Phormio of Terence, Vat. Lat. 3868, folio 84v

Making a point at the start of the speech

Added emphasis*

Exhortation or reproach

*Miniature for act 5, scene 2, lines 767—98, from the illustrated manuscript of the Hecyra of Terence, Vat. Lat. 3868, folio 75r

Presenting a logic jump

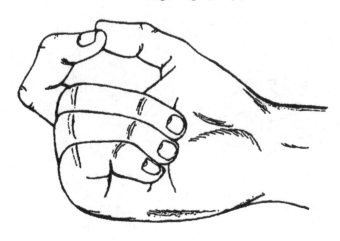

Drawing attention

Aversion

Modesty

Argument

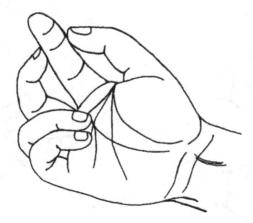

Wonder

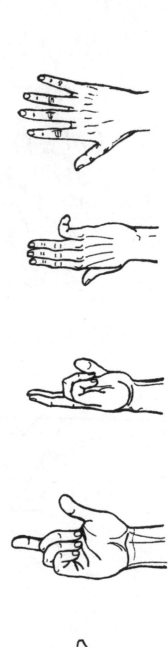
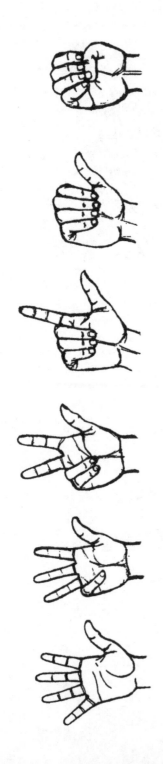

Adoration

Horror

Grief

Exhortation

Gestures were for all

In the early Roman empire, gestures became a tool for both speakers and the audience. They were a part of the two-way communication process (explored further in Chapter 2). Gestures could enhance or supplement words or even take the place of words, providing the nonverbal communication component. In the same way, they enhanced the listener's experience, giving them more insight and emotion, and creating a path for that emotion to communicate back to the orator as the audience utilised their own gestures and responses—such as bricks, tiles and bees—to show agreement or disagreement.

Gestures Today

When I think about gestures today I turn to the term 'dichotomous thinking', also known as black-and-white thinking. This is when your thought patterns assign things into one of two categories—either 'good' or 'bad'. Black-and-white thinking is part of a group of thinking patterns called cognitive distortions—and I can think of no better example of cognitive distortion than the way we consider the use of the hands and arms in communication.

All babies are born using their arms to gesture, and young children become quickly proficient at pointing, reaching up and clenching their fists to show they want something, as well as learning the gestures that their elders use. For example, little Prince Louis stole the show at Trooping the Colour in England in 2023, throwing his arms high and saluting. As a little boy it is all part of life. Then we go to school and are told to 'stand still' or 'stop fidgeting'. 'You gesture too much!' the student is told by the teacher, and in one fell swoop, they feel silly and belittled.

Sadly, when children are told off for moving, gesturing or fidgeting too much, they become stifled. They don't know why they need to be static, which undermines their confidence. Crippling our gestures cripples our creative spirit.

As adults, my clients try desperately to hold their hands still and make no movement, which is rarely something a person moving freely would consider. Sometimes they sit with their hands under the table; sometimes they sit on their hands, with their elbows tightly squeezed to their bodies and their hands clenched firmly, or with their fists tightly clenched at the centre of their body. They become stiffer and more stifled. They lose the power in their body, they stop breathing and their voice starts to shake. In the same way as they say 'the hip bone's connected to the thigh bone...', one disaster begets another.

Modern repetitive patterns emerge from stifled gestures

The unwritten and unspoken laws of corporate boardrooms and workplaces over the last 70 years suggest that hand use in the form of gestures is not required and can show unnecessary distraction and a lack of professionalism. This is patently untrue. But because we stifle our natural gestures, we see some patterns emerge that actually may be distracting and unprofessional.

Think about it now. What do you do when you communicate? How do you sit? What are your unspoken rules?

Whenever you choose to hinder your natural gestures and movements, it can lead to repetition because we are stifled into a limiting range of behaviours. And what I have noticed over the years is that each of us seems to have a slightly different repetitive pattern.

- **The snap.** When the arms and hands open, the fists snap to a clench almost immediately and the arms and elbows also snap back into the centre of the body with haste.

- **The penguin.** When the arms are long and locked by our sides and just the hands flick out from the side of the body, I call this 'the penguin' because it looks like a penguin flapping its wings as it walks.

- **Windscreen wipers.** When the hands are folded across the body and one lower arm flicks up and down at right angles, I call this the 'windscreen wipers' gesture because it reflects the motion of the wipers of a car during rain.

- **The *Tyrannosaurus rex*.** When the arms are held tightly to the body and the hands form a fist on the upper chest, sometimes the hands just flick open and shut, like the ancient short-armed monster.

- **The flashing figleaf.** The worst repetitive action is when we hold the arms long and clenched over our groin, opening the hands up as we speak.

Unlike well thought out and useful gestures, these are distracting for the listener and for the speaker themselves. These incongruent gestures are often a depiction of stress rather than any real mode of communication, and act as a misdirection that distracts the listener from the true message.

The more time that the listener spends trying to read the nonverbal gestures, the more these outshine the words themselves, leading to more confusion as the listener is taken in by the meaningless nature of the repetitive stress pattern of the hands.

These incongruent gestures are also distracting to the speaker themself, and these unconscious stress patterns reinforce performance anxiety (essentially 'stage fright'). Again, when you experience performance anxiety, it impacts your ability to communicate, to stay on message and certainly to engage with your audience, all of which can negatively affect your career, your life, your self-esteem and your self-confidence, and impact your ability to lead with gravitas.

Lastly, locked arms (the Penguin gesture, windscreen wipers and others) are simply a way of holding the breath. So, when you lock your arms, you are not only distracting the listener but you are also distracting yourself and, like a cherry on the cake, you can't seem to catch your breath. This is hardly a pattern that will instil trust or respect and consequently is a total blockage to gravitas.

A personal experience with gestures

From my career as a singer, I learned that elbows stuck to your body mean you cannot breathe! Elbows stuck to the body and fists clenched were seen in my singing time with Professor Ellen Müller-Preis as corresponding to a jammed diaphragm, leading to poor vocal outcomes.

Not only do tightly held elbows and fists jam the diaphragm, but this in turn leads to rapid, shallow breathing (known as a 'high breath'). A high breath leads to less oxygen, and less oxygen (20 per cent of the oxygen needed) leads to brain freeze.

So there you are, standing before your team, your elbows tightly jammed to your body, and suddenly you cannot think. This is unhealthy, ineffective and damaging to your self-esteem, and it all goes back to the way you have been conditioned throughout your life to limit your gestures.

But when this happens, we tend to think our failing is something externally related. Maybe the group doesn't like you? Maybe you don't know enough about your topic? Maybe you simply don't deserve to be there? These are the kinds of thoughts that lead directly to performance anxiety and imposter syndrome.

However, this is rarely the case. Instead, it's simply that the way we hold our bodies stops them from becoming a natural expression of our speaking. To combat these thoughts (which are generally not real or representative of reality), we need to rethink the use of gestures. Maybe the solution is to get your arms off your body, flatten your palms and start breathing again. But we need to learn how by considering what went wrong, why we have lost the use of gestures and how we can bring gestures back into the way we communicate.

What went wrong?

Modern notions around gestures have clearly led us to a difficult situation. Yet, the ancients seemed to have it right (and that focus on gestures remained in place for almost 2000 years). So, where did things go wrong?

The classic textbook *The Communication Skills Handbook*[12] claims that it will 'equip contemporary students with the written and oral communication guidelines you need to succeed at university and beyond'. Yet, there is no mention of gestures playing any role in those communications. It then goes on to say its features include 'specific information relating to the usage of ePortfolios, Wikis and Weblogs for assessment'.

It is strongly suggestive of how we all see 'communication' through a different lens and that students are expected to learn the use of gestures through an online format.

In the healthcare sector, the book *Communication: Core Interpersonal Skills for Healthcare*[13] hints at something more akin to our topic. The contents tell us it provides:

- effective conclusions of interactions and services: negotiating closure

- remote telecommunication.

However, there's no mention of gestures here either.

And so I turn to the popular *For Dummies* series and the excellent *Communication Skills For Dummies*.[14] In the voluminous 369 pages, there are 41 uses of the word 'gesture', but mostly to say that you should use 'gestures and facial expressions to support your spoken message' and to admonish the reader to 'read gestures in clusters'. But there are no clues as to what this means in practice.

Even in the contemporary rhetoric-focused textbook *The Rhetoric Companion*,[15] out of the 156 pages, gestures cover a general discussion over one page.

Birdwhistell[16] wrote of gestures, but I hear little reference to it in my corporate travels.

These are just a couple of examples, but I could continue endlessly demonstrating that gesturing is barely documented in contemporary leadership literature.

Furthermore, with the rise of virtual communication, the hands may as well have been dismembered. With virtual communications (such as on a video call), the amount of use we are giving gestures in our communications is almost non-existent. Where we may have used our hands — even in unconscious gestures — while standing and speaking in front of someone in person, when we are online, we tend to sit very still, keeping our hands completely out of the frame.

When experts participate in explorations of nonverbal communication in the virtual space, they give us extremely limited suggestions that we use a nod to communicate agreement, and a wave to say goodbye.[17] Other experts, bemoaning the fact that the audience is disengaged, replying to text messages on their phones or working on their computers during online meetings, suggest that we stand during virtual communications so that we can better incorporate our whole bodies when speaking. Yet we're given no suggestions as to the best use of gestures in this space (or any other).[18]

I am left again wondering how this gaping hole in our modern understanding of communication delivery came about.

Why did we lose gestures?

To understand the loss of gestures, it is helpful to consider when the use of gestures in communication changed within our time.

Ancient and medieval writers, from Augustine (354–430 CE)[19] to Amalarius of Metz (775–850 CE)[20] and Hugh of Saint-Victor (1096–1141 CE),[21] emphasised the role of gesture in effective speaking and preaching. Evidence can be found in historical artefacts over time. One can also find references to gesture in artist representations in bronze and marble sculptures, on state and private reliefs and on coins. These demonstrate that the rhetorical vocabulary of gesture was an essential component of the delivery of speeches of the ancients.

It appears the interest in rhetorical gestures as reflected in history abruptly ceased in the last decade of the 19th century. In fact, there are no extended treatments of the subject at all between the year 1892 and the 1980s, and there may be a couple of reasons for that omission.

THE MEGAPHONE

The first proposition is that this startling gap in what had been, up to this point, a continuous and lively topic of scholarly enquiry, is that it exactly coincides with the widespread use of the electric microphone and amplifier in speechmaking.

It is believed the current pervasive use of the microphone and amplifier has rendered gesture partially redundant as a form of communication as it appears, when our voices grew louder, our gestures and body language, in general, became less of a focus.

However, while our verbal reach may be larger, we have lost something in the process. Audiences have become conditioned to focus on listening rather than watching. They have begun to regard the message as more important than the messenger. And that has undermined our modern ability to learn these important skills, which, in turn, has undermined our overall confidence in speaking, delivering on stage and even leading. In other words, today we lack *gravitas*.

THE NAZI CONNECTION

It is my contention that another added deterrent was the use of gestures by Hitler during the Second World War. It struck me that, given many of my teachers in Europe were already in their 80s when I worked with them, they were German and had been brought up in an era of gestures.

What I discovered was that Germania, an apparently harmless description of the territories, customs and tribes of Germany by 1st century Roman historian Cornelius Tacitus (56–120 CE), was acclaimed by Nazi Germans as a banner. They believed that it drew a portrait of the desired Aryan—'virtuous, fearless and heavily militarized'—qualities the Nazis felt had reverberated through the centuries and supported the racial identity of the modern German.[22]

Hitler's obsession with ancient Rome led him to adopt many of their practices—among these, gesturing. He practised his gestures in an exaggerated way to cope with his need to motivate a large group of people at once through his speeches, and what became known as the Hitler salute or the Sieg Heil salute (see overleaf) was a use of the ancient Roman greeting that has become his best-known example.[23]

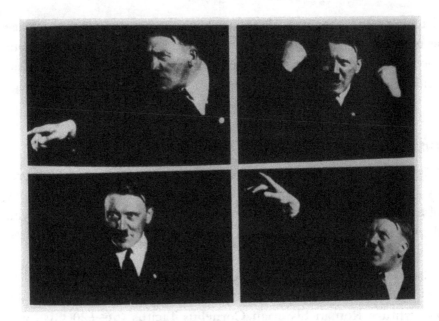

Hitler practising different gestures.

Hitler's use of the camera was fascinating for its time, but examining oneself in motion was never a new concept and something already documented in ancient Greece:

Demosthenes used to study action while looking into a large mirror, and though the polished surface made the right side of the body appear the left, he could notwithstanding trust his eyes for the effect which he would be enabled to produce.[24]

My work in the opera led me to learn about and embrace gestures in my communications. But in retrospect, my hunch was that I had been given the gift of gesturing that few had experienced. Distilling my ideas, I began to question if this gift was somehow falsely associated with a Nazi connection, when, in fact, its origin was ancient Rome.

Alexander Mariotto, an expert on the Gladiators of ancient Rome, points out the link between 'Nazis, history and Romans'.[25] Mariotto notes that Hitler adopted the gestures and symbols of ancient Rome via the Italian dictator Benito Mussolini and tells a wonderful story of the making of the movie *Gladiator*, directed by Ridley Scott, where the gestures of the actor Russell Crowe were edited for fear of a Nazi association.

In the movie, the character of the gladiator addresses his warriors and, while aloft on his warrior horse, gives the gesture of the Emperor, stretching his hand upwards and forwards to the right. This movement was cut and replaced by a clenched fist to the chest.

These exaggerated gestures have become repulsive because they've somehow become associated with a Nazi mindset. However, gestures did not originate in German politics. Hitler stole them from the ancient Romans.

What can we do?

So many of my clients share that they have been told they 'gesture too much', so they believe the solution is to simply stop gesturing. But this has left us with big gaps in our communications (and, therefore, our ability to communicate with gravitas).

The skill of gesture offers unmatched opportunities for creating better communication on the stage and when delivering in any forum. Much of this has been lost, but some modern scholars are working to return this to common usage.

One fascinating study from the beginning of the 19th century attempts to recreate the gestures of Roman actors by observing and analysing the gestures of contemporary Neapolitans as observed in everyday life on the streets of Naples. The contention here is that the modern Neopolitans use gestures profusely in a congruent and meaningful way and that this activity has stemmed from a continuous timeline over 2000 years. In Andrea de Jorio's 1832 treatise, *La mimica degli antichi investigata nel gestire napoletano* ('The body language of the ancients as interpreted in Neapolitan gesture'), he contends that gestures tend to remain stable over time and that therefore he could reconstruct ancient body language by closely observing Neapolitan contemporaries.[26]

If the gestures remain stable, then so too should our interpretation and understanding of those gestures remain stable. Modern-day leaders should feel confident that using them within their own speeches and delivery will serve to enhance their communication with their staff and their audience in general.

How does it work?

One of my clients was an international CEO whose company had a team that had experienced a dangerous episode where many people had lost their lives in a workplace accident. Facing the media was a hugely stressful event and he was understandably distraught. But he was also keen to let the public know the circumstances and the response.

Working on the skills for this interview, gestures played a critical role. We worked out a gesture for the key message and gestures that led into that key message. While it is hard to describe on paper, let me assure you this was congruent, non-repetitive and told a story. Not only did it free the body for breath and help with stress, but the gesturing helped him understand his space when he spoke and worked as a strong memory technique under stress.

Another client I worked with suffered quite severe performance anxiety and, as I often hear, was threatening to resign her job if she had to present or do media (which was an essential part of the role).

Analysing her repetitive patterns, we realised that she was holding her arms tight against her body and when she moved them away, she'd continually snap her hands back into a clenched position (I refer to this as 'the snap' earlier in this chapter!). While this sounds extreme, it is such a common pattern that we can become blind to it and to the damage it can cause to communications between the message and the speaker.

Working through the change process, I realised that there was no point in asking her (or anyone) to stop repeating a gesture, particularly one that's become so ingrained. It's better to build a repertoire of movement that can be drawn on and to practise these new gestures over and over and over until they become part of who we are.

Today, this client remembers all her presentations by associating gestures with key points. Like a choreographed dance piece, gestures have played a major role in freeing the body of physical stress and also providing a strong guide to memory and pre-empting what comes next.

Modern Use of Gestures

In a world where achieving gravitas is considered a sought-after goal to help us lead, to help us be effective and to help build our own confidence, we need our hands more than ever. We need them to communicate critical messages. We need them to work as a technique for promoting our memory and we need them to free our own bodies so that we can breathe. One phrase we used as singers was that the body never 'runs out of breath'. Instead, the body 'runs into tension' and gesturing is a major tool for releasing that tension.

So what do we do with our hands? If we aren't going to keep them still or repetitively move them backwards and forwards, what are the choices?

The three golden rules of gestures

Firstly, it is simple when you consider these three golden rules.

Gestures are:

1. non-repetitive

2. congruent (aligns with the words being spoken)

3. held (until the next movement).

Each of these golden rules are important when using gestures. When gestures are uniquely used (non-repetitive) they give more weight and meaning to the words you're speaking. Holding them between movements allows you to use gestures as both a memory aid and helps you to keep your body and breath free from natural tensions that might creep in.

But it is this notion of congruence that draws our attention back to ancient Rome. Anciently, gestures were prescriptive (determined by the expectations of the time), both in the movements themselves and in the messaging they would convey. While there was a general continuity of gestures throughout the period, there is evidence that they became increasingly complex over time, particularly during the Imperial age.[27]

THE HANDSHAKE

Consider the handshake. This is a greeting style used by most people today, even past the COVID-19 pandemic. In fact, the handshake has been around for approximately 3000 years, and is even depicted in drawings found on ancient Greek vases.

Think about how you shake someone's hand. It is not necessarily about the hand. Which leg do you send forward? Where is your weight? Is your arm long or bent? Do you strike forwards or karate chop down? Is the grip firm or weak, and where are your eyes?

We can find answers to these questions from ancient times. Consider this: the handshake is a sword thrust without the sword, so the thrust is forwards. The weight is on the front leg, which is actually the right leg with the right hand. The arm is long, and the pressure of the hand is in the thrust between the thumb and second finger. Lastly, the eyes are on the eyes of the person you are greeting.

WONDER

The gesture of expressing wonder is as relevant today as it was in ancient Rome.

This gesture is one of the more complicated, because, like the handshake, it involves movement. To make a gesture of wonder, the orator would hold up the right hand, with all the fingers extended, and then curl the fingers back into the palm one by one beginning with the little finger.

Once all the fingers have been brought back to the palm, the movement is then reversed by opening the fingers again but in the opposite sequence while at the same time gently rotating the entire hand.

THE GREETING

Another gesture we learn from ancient Rome is one depicting open arms (the 'greeting' gesture). Many depictions of orators show them with their arms thrown wide. This gesture is one that demonstrates trust. Generally the arms are held at waist or chest height with the palms reaching forward.

This gesture was used widely in ancient Rome and is still used by today's modern orators, particularly in the political fields. (see below).

Depiction of the 'greeting' gesture being used by an ancient Roman orator in the Senate.

Former US President Donald Trump using the 'greeting' gesture in a speech.

This gesture is still used throughout recent history and even today in an attempt to engender those same feelings of trust and even believability.

Gestures of the hands

When considering modern gestures, we start with gestures of our hands. With our hands we can ask, promise, call people to us and send them away, threaten, supplicate or intimate dislike or fear. We can also use our hands to signify joy, grief, doubt, acknowledgement or penitence, and even to indicate measure, quantity, number and time.[29]

1. POINTING

Pointing was and is a powerful gesture that could convey both positive and negative meanings. It is one of the most used gestures of the modern era, but not always with good results. How often do we teach our youth that 'it's rude to point'?

In ancient Rome, it was also a highly used gesture. Pointing could be done with any finger, but never with the thumb. If an orator pointed to a thing, place or person then they didn't need to also use words. The gesture replaced those words, rendering them moot.

If an orator pointed to a building or the background, this was often loaded with symbolic meaning or powerful associations. For example, he might point to a cult statue to allude to the virtues associated with that deity.

2. LISTING

Whenever you describe a list, you have several options. You could use the fingers: holding up one finger for the number 1, two fingers for the number 2, and so on.

Or you could do what I call 'walk like an Egyptian'. This involves bending your arm at the elbow to the side of your body and bending the hand at right angles away from your body then moving it down to describe the points.

You can also mark three spaces along an imagined horizontal line in front of your body, or you could move forward away from your body's current position, each move aligning with one item on the list.

There you go: you now have four different options for describing a list!

3. A PINCH

This movement shows you pinching your thumb and forefinger together with just a small space between. This demonstrates that something is very small.

4. CLENCHED HAND

Using a solid fist, shaking it or even punching it in the air, demonstrates intensity—that the point you are making is very important—or an emotion, such as anger or frustration.

5. EVERYTHING

The 'everything gesture' is done by sweeping two hands across your body and out from the centre, one right and one left. It shows that your words are encompassing everything.

6. MAGNANIMITY

The gesture that demonstrates that you are magnanimous (generous or forgiving) is when you throw your arms wide with your head back while facing your audience. Use this when making a grand gesture.

7. GROWTH

The 'growth' gesture is done by moving your hand upwards to indicate an increase. You can use this for growth or direction, or even for excitement.

8. THE 'YOU' GESTURE

A simple gesture of reaching out towards your listener with the palm facing upwards to indicate that you're referring to that person.

9. THE 'ME' GESTURE

Another simple gesture of using your hand pressed against your chest to indicate that you're referencing yourself.

10. THE 'COME TOGETHER' GESTURE

Bringing both hands together with fingers interlaced symbolically demonstrates two things coming together as one. The key here is to have the elbows off the body so the line between the elbows through the hands is a straight line.

These are only a small number of the gestures that you can be using to improve your nonverbal communications and, therefore, gravitas.

Writing: a modern adaptation

Given the notion that respect is seen by having the head and hand in the same direction, let's consider writing on the board. Think how one normally writes, or perhaps indicates towards a PowerPoint. Most people will gesture with the hand and turn their head to the audience, which, if they follow the ancients, is a sign of disrespect.

Instead, the idea is to keep the head and hand facing the same direction when communicating and to only speak when facing the audience.

This technique to draw the attention of the audience to the board, turn your head and arm back to the audience and then, and only then, to talk, has become colloquially known as 'touch, turn and talk'.

Practice exercise

Using these elements, and increasing your ability to communicate, will increase your feelings of confidence. As your confidence increases, your fear of performing will lessen, and your overall gravitas will be elevated.

Consider Tesla's mission statement, 'To accelerate the world's transition to sustainable energy.' Try gesturing to Tesla's mission statements. Remember there is no right answer. Be creative. Get your elbows off your body.

An example may be to roll the hands around each other quickly in front of the body to represent action, then to take the right arm out to the future position and then draw the flat hand across in a straight line, as if painting on glass to represent the writing of the words 'sustainable energy'. This is three separate gestures, one with hands in front of the body , one with the arm moving out and up to the right and one with the hand and upper arm drawing the goal in the sky. Of course, this is just one option. Another may be to sweep the arm out to the right and reach up to the sky. The point is that the mission statement is enhanced by associating it with a congruent gesture.

Here are some other gestures to consider.

Gestures of the eyes

> *As for keeping [the eyes] fully or partially closed while speaking, surely none save an uneducated man or a fool would dream of doing such a thing.*[30]

— Quintilian

It often surprises those that I work with to learn that the way eyes were used in ancient Rome were seen as gestures. In essence, ancient Romans felt that the eyes were the most expressive part of the face, so one of the most important parts of nonverbal communication.

Quintilian says of the eyes:

But what is most expressive in the face is the eye, through which the mind chiefly manifests itself, insomuch that the eyes, even while they remain motionless, can sparkle with joy or contract a gloomy look under sadness. To the eyes, also, nature has given tears, which are the interpreters of our feelings and which burst forth in grief or trickle gently down in joy. But when the eyes are in motion, they assume an appearance of eagerness, disregard, pride, sternness, mildness, or threatening, all of which will be manifested in the eyes of an orator as his subject shall require.[31]

The ancient writers and orators believed that eyes could be used to the best effect to produce expressions that allowed the audience to feel what the speaker felt, and engage with the speaker's message. Quintilian advises that they shouldn't be 'rigid and distended, languid or torpid, wanton or rolling, nor should they ever seem to swim or look watery with pleasure, or glance sideways, or appear, as it were, amorous, or as if they were asking or promising something'.[32] And, of course, he would expect that you would never close your eyes when speaking to your audience.

The ancients also believed in the power of the eyebrows, which can show anger by contraction, sadness by lowering, and cheerfulness by expansion, and of the use of the 'blood', which can show our emotions and feelings to the audience in a truly nonverbal way. (Today we'd think of this as blushing from shame or embarrassment, when the blood rushes into our face; or when the blood drains away, showing a pale, waxy expression as fear.)

The eyes also help us when we are using other types of gestures. Typically, the eyes of the orator would follow the movement, which shows the audience that they are in harmony with the gesture's communication. Of course, if their eyes moved opposite to the gesture, the orator might be indicating that they actually disagreed or were averse to the facts of opinion being communicated.[33]

Sometimes eye contact can be considered aggressive. However, research shows that the key to softening the eyes is to have movement. This may be through nodding, changing the shape of the face through smiling or, the most important aspect, blinking.[34] Researchers have even studied the best blink rate (which they found to be 15 blinks per minute for the look of 'listening')![35]

All of this can lead to very soft eye contact, which ameliorates any fear of coming across as aggressive. (In fact, the softness of eye contact may be an area women can lead the way in the new era. More on this in Chapter 6.)

But again, despite the fulsome lessons we're learning from ancient Rome, we aren't taught about eye movement and communication today. How often have you been speaking to someone and noticed that they don't ever make eye contact—even briefly? Or when sitting in an audience, do you notice that the speaker looks away or off into the distance and never seems to engage their audience—or worse, delivers with a flat, expressionless look on their face?

Summary

Gestures were a foundational skill for mankind in Western culture right up until the end of the 19th century. After the Second World War, the understanding and implementation of gestures in our lives as a crucial communication tool simply died.

The ancient Romans have given fine examples of why, where and how to gesture, and these are easily introduced in the modern world when we follow our three golden rules: ensure gestures are congruent, non-repetitive and held.

The eyes, an area considered by the Romans to be another tool of gesture, are something we need to bring under our control. Yes, eye gestures vary from culture to culture, and by having them under control we're better able to create nonverbal communication with our listeners.

All of this aligns to create a two-way communication that instils trust and respect and, therefore, gravitas.

Chapter 5
Voice

*God, that all-powerful Creator of nature and architecture of
the world, has impressed man with no character so proper to
distinguish him from other animals, as by the faculty of speech.*[1]

— Quintilian

**Does your voice shake under stress? Do you have difficulty
being heard in meetings? Have you given up trying to interject
because your voice is too small?**

Well, blow all your troubles away, because all of these statements are
misleading. Voices don't shake, people do; techniques exist that can
help you be heard; and voices do not come in different sizes. Everyone
(who doesn't have a vocal injury or experience speech difficulties)
has a voice perfect to fulfil every vocal need.

Unfortunately, if you're like many people, you may not understand
that you have the perfect instrument within your grasp. And believing
your voice is below par can be shattering. Everybody is vulnerable to
personal, social and physically imposed stresses, and over time these
stresses initiate habitual, intricate brain patterns that can be reflected
in our posture, breath and voice.

The Romans understood this mind-body-voice connection well. They got that voice is about freeing the body. They also knew that the voice reflects the stresses of a whole life and that vocal dynamics can be said to both echo and amplify psychodynamics. They took that challenge head on and found ways to minimise the impact of these stressors.

If you feel your voice is failing you, this can have a spiralling effect on your confidence. A lack of confidence, in turn, brings on patterns of vocal behaviour that undermine trust and respect from others. In other words, the lack of a strong voice contributes to your own lack of gravitas.

Voice is important. It sounds obvious, but somehow that message just does not sink in these days. No matter where I look, working with the deep and complicated area of voice seems to be hindered by the disparate fields of the vocal, body and 'communication' professions—none of which consciously address voice for the everyday voice user.

Before we dive into the fundamentals of the voice and gravitas, think about how much work you have done on your voice. The answer for most people is little, or even none. Possibly this is because it is hard to know where to start, even where you recognise that you could use some help strengthening your speaking voice. For the Greeks and Romans, however, this training started young.

One contemporary communication book offered this advice on speaking too softly: 'Only women have problems with voice' it read, with the startling advice to 'use a microphone'![2] This is misleading and, to my mind, just simply wrong. Women are not the only ones who struggle with public speaking, and using a microphone is a temporary solution with no long-term benefit that brings a hell of a lot of risk into play.

Is it not a risk to leave your development to the vagaries of an electrical appliance? On one occasion, I went to give a keynote at a conference in an abandoned warehouse, which the organisers thought was incredibly trendy. It was, until the electrical system failed. A few speakers, who had even travelled from overseas, were left struggling to project and let down the client at their time of need. On a personal level, I have had young mothers tell me of the fear of not being able to call out to their children in danger in the park as they head dangerously towards the road.

You also may be resisting voice training, and for good reason. In contemporary Western society, we have a set of models that leads us to believe we are stuck with the voice we have. We don't believe it can be changed and we talk about the voice as having a mind of its own. It does not.

The poor old voice becomes a scapegoat for a plethora of inadequacies—lack of preparation or a failure to understand our audiences—but we blame the voice. We treat it like a separate entity that we are born with that we cannot change, and over which we have no control. And because we believe we cannot change, we stop trying to make those changes that could lead to better leadership.

However, this hasn't always been the case. The ancients knew that 'voice is a choice!', not just the sound you're born with, and, through my own work, I know it to be true as well.

My interest in voice is not just an interest; it has been a passion since I was a child. And through my studies, as well as through decades of professional practice, none of that passion has dwindled. I have learned a lot, including that we can all be confident and that a magnificent voice is within our grasp, and all of this understanding is encapsulated in the knowledge of the ancients.

The Romans and Voice

Thousands of years ago, the ancients were steeped in a history where 'voice is one of the oldest areas of study'.[3] In fact, singing was not considered separately from speech—together, they were considered from the perspectives of physiological and psychological connection.

Reflecting the psychological connection of an individual to their voice, the word *personality* is believed to have derived from the Latin *persona*, which originally meant the mouthpiece of the mask used by actors.[4] That sound, inextricably linked with the person, passed through the hole at the mouth of the mask to reach its audience.

Similarly, the term *psyche* was derived from an older Greek term, *psychein*, which meant 'to breathe' or 'to blow' (which would make a sound).[5] This etymology demonstrates that, to the ancients, mind, body and sound were one.

The intertwining of the physical and psychological perspectives were therefore inherent in the early understanding of voice. And, in some cultures, a deep, all-encompassing and critical life force was recognised from the voice, as it still is in the classical-singing training tradition.

The ancient Romans had none of the scientific knowledge we have today, but they inherited a wealth of wisdom about the voice and were far more aware of its use and capability.

While practising in Athens in the 3rd century BC, Aristotle suggested that the voice was produced in the trachea and larynx by the impact of air and that this process was inspired by the soul, which Aristotle located in the heart and lungs—therefore demonstrating a clear connection to breath and emotion. In the 13th century, there still existed a strong belief that the vocal system was a derivative of some emotional origin—this time, from the heart.[6]

(It's interesting to note that the Greek physician Claudius Galen—born in 129 CE and considered the founder of laryngology—had correctly identified the larynx as the instrument of voice production.[7] His framing of the larynx as the source of *principalissimum organum vocis*—which literally means 'beautiful singing'—although a physiological breakthrough, also marked the beginning of a split in the science of vocal studies, with one side focused on physical elements and the other on emotional or mental elements. This split has impacted our study of voice and has influenced how we understand the role of the voice in the way we communicate today.)[8]

Of Quintilian's 170 statements on delivery, a large proportion are voice-related, and this is because of the inextricable link of voice to gesture and everything 'delivery'. Key to the study of voice by the ancients was the fascination with the diaphragm as the source of the voice. I often say to my clients 'all roads lead to Rome', and by this I mean that everything goes back to the diaphragm.

The Romans worked on their voices, building their vocal skills and capabilities—they never assumed that a strong voice was a given. While their methods may seem somewhat flawed to us today (it was said that 'Nero drank dried boar's dung and slept with weights on his diaphragm'[9]), the focus they placed on the importance of voice is one that we should certainly be emulating in the way we communicate today.

The Romans and volume

One of the things the ancient Romans understood was the power of the voice, particularly in terms of the volume of the voice.

Emperors knew that it was possible to clearly hear a single speaker at about 65 metres in an open space with average background noise. At the 65-metre mark, heralds were then placed to call out the key messages or ask for silence, and beyond that, when extremes of distance were reached, the Romans backed up their speaking volume with yet more heralds who circulated carrying large placards that conveyed the main messages to the rest of the audience. For the Romans, being heard was critical.

But for a distance of up to 65 metres, the Romans relied on the natural volume of the speaker alone! To a modern speaker, that distance seems inconceivable. In fact, I recently had someone ask me to help them with microphone technique for six people in a room!

Of course, the Romans also recognised that the carrying ability of an individual's voice was not entirely dependent on volume, but on a combination of natural tonal quality and training.[10] They were able to achieve this carrying ability through volume as well as the body and the body's posture—movement of the body was never seen as separate to the making of sound.

Connection to the body

For the Romans, voice and body were inextricably linked. Quintilian made it clear that 'there are many things...necessary...such as strength of body, for instance, that the voice may not dwindle...bodily strength can be maintained by walking, anointing with oil, continence, and easy digestion of food, which is the result of moderation in eating.'[11]

In Chapter 3, I talked about how the body can be seen as an instrument for producing sound. Here, we can see just how closely the Romans viewed the body and the voice, even when talking about bodily fatigue. The Romans felt that fatigue, 'affects the voice as it affects the whole body, not for the present merely, but for some time afterwards.'[12]

I've seen this in my own work with Professor Müller-Preis. She would suggest that before a performance, it would be better to run around the block to warm up the body than to stand in a room repeating scales. In other words, warming up the body as a whole will get you further than just warming up the voice alone. While Professor Müller-Preis was speaking about singing, this is equally true for speaking generally.

The Romans and pitch

Pitch for the Romans was part of the musicality of performance. According to Quintilian,

Delivery is considered elegant if it is supported by a voice that is easy, powerful, fine, flexible, firm, sweet, well-sustained, clear, and pure, and that cuts the air and penetrates the ear, for there is a kind of voice naturally qualified to make itself heard, not by its strength, but by a peculiar excellence of tone.[13]

The only limits on pitch, Quintilian further explained, were that 'Neither the lowest musical tone, nor the highest, is proper for oratory.' This does not mean that high- or low-pitched voices are 'bad', just that they don't carry as well in an amphitheatre.

When it comes to pitch, the Romans believed that the key was to have a voice that has range and flexibility: 'It is a voice obedient to the will of the speaker, capable of every variety of sound and inflection that can be required, and possessed, as they say, of all the notes of a musical instrument.'[14] The Romans worked to develop that flexibility and fluidity in pitch that led to a voice that was natural and authentic-sounding while still having the volume to carry as far as possible.

The relationship to singing

The Romans also believed that speaking and singing voices were of the same cut and required similar development. As we see from Quintilian's quote that follows, the ancients believed that orators didn't have to be as excessive in their training as singers, but it was essential that they work on the same areas to develop the voice (albeit to a lesser degree):[15]

> *Though exercise is necessary alike for singing teachers and orators, in order that all their faculties may be in full vigour, the same kind of attention to the body is not to be expected from both because regular times for walking cannot be scheduled by a man who is occupied in so many duties of civil life. Nor can he tune his voice at leisure from the lowest to the highest notes, or give it rest when he pleases from the labours of the forum, since he has often to speak on many trials in succession. Nor need he observe the same care in regard to diet.*

Quintilian also gives us some insight how the speaking voice of orators would differ from the singing voice of performers, and the endurance the practice would require:

> *We need not so much a soft and sweet voice as one that is strong and durable, and though singers may soften all sounds, even the highest, by a certain modulation of the voice, we, on the contrary, must often speak with roughness and vehemence. Also, we must frequently watch whole nights, we must imbibe the smoke of the lamp by which we study, and we must remain long, during the day, in garments moistened with perspiration. Let us not, therefore, weaken our voice by delicate treatment of ourselves or bring it to a condition which will not be enduring.[16]*

The message here is that while speaking has less demands than singing, and there is no need for vast vocal training, it is still a demanding practice. Manage your body and you will manage your sound.

The Romans and authenticity

With regard to authenticity, I am sometimes asked if you should speak the same on stage as off, to which I reply there would be something wrong if you did not! Quintilian reinforces this by saying,

> *I consider the best kind of exercise for the voice, when it is well strengthened and developed, to be that which has most resemblance to the orator's business, namely, to speak every day just as we plead in the forum, for by this means, not only the voice and lungs will be strengthened, but a graceful carriage of the body will be acquired, suited to our style of speaking.*[17]

There was no 'fake it to make it' ideal in ancient Rome. Romans weren't expected to act differently on stage (beyond the elements of oratory performance) than in real life by changing their voice or demeanour to something inauthentic and unnatural. All changes when it came to voice and delivery were for the improvement of the individual and to accentuate the message being delivered. Vocal and delivery training in practice was more than an act of professional development; it was intertwined with personal development, with the idea to increase the authenticity of the speaker's own voice rather than alter their voice altogether. Perhaps this is why gravitas was so much better understood during this time — because those who delivered with authenticity were more trusted overall.

Voice and change

For the Romans, the voice was malleable. Quintilian says, 'The good qualities of the voice, like those of all our other faculties, are improved by attention and deteriorated by neglect.'[18] How we treat our voice, and work on its development, can help it to grow stronger or weaker (in terms of delivery, rather than in terms of volume or pitch).

Changes in the voice, for the ancients, also occurred every time they spoke. The ancients did not speak of consciously altering their pitch, pace or volume, although these are desirable outcomes. Instead, they spoke of how to alter the voice for the best effect while delivering a speech. As Quintilian wondered, 'For example, must not the words "unhappy man, poor creature," be uttered in a low and subdued tone, and must not "courageous, vehement, robber," be spoken in a more elevated and energetic tone?'[19] The emphasis was on the energy of the body—including gestures and posture—and the requirements of the message itself, which was reflected in the resulting vocal tone.

On altering the voice, Quintilian does not suggest altering its pitch, pace or volume consciously in speech.[20] Instead, he claims that we need to embrace the range of our vocal capacity by practising varying texts to test and expand the limits. He advises orators of the time, which is equally good advice to modern communicators, to exercise the voice by learning passages from books by heart, and then turning these into speeches with the accompanying emphasis and emotion. Quintilian also suggests using passages from books on a wide variety of subjects, which will give the speaker the opportunity to prepare 'for every mode of speaking'. This, Quintilian says, 'will be sufficient exercise'.[21]

Key takeaway from the Romans on voice

The key takeaway from the Romans is that we should be embracing the study of an underlying universal style of communication that is deeply connected to emotion and embraces a wide spectrum of vocal sound.

The challenge with voice from this perspective is a complicated intertwining of the psychological and physical, which lends itself more to *unlearning*, rather than *learning*. Just as we needed to *unlearn* the limitations on gestures that we've been taught previously (stand still, don't move your hands!), we also need to *unlearn* many of the ideas we currently believe about voice (you're stuck with your voice, it cannot change, this means you can never really have gravitas!). On the other hand, if we can approach the gifts of our born perfection (our perfect voices) with an adult's understanding broadened by the ancient's perspective (in other words, that gravitas comes from training our natural voices rather than arising from the few voices that are in some way born superior) then we're in a much better position to make the changes we need to embrace voice in our communications.

Voice Today

Before we consider the voice in today's world, ask yourself these questions:

- Do you speak on the breath in or the breath out?

- Do you understand how you initiate sound?

- Can you see what makes you loud and why your voice sometimes won't work?

My first experiences of voice in the corporate arena frankly shocked me. I was surprised at the overall ignorance of vocal production, vocal health and vocal summoning power. The vast majority of people outside the vocal professions have no idea about what to do when their 'voice' goes wrong or how to utilise it to its best.

Going back to the questions, did you know the answers? I imagine not, and that's fine. How could you know how to answer these questions when voice is simply not part of our modern-day discussion about communication?

Consider this everyday, real-life example. Walking into a shop one day, I placed my groceries on the counter to be greeted by the very sweet assistant in an inaudible vocal fry. A *vocal fry* happens when there is virtually no air coming out of your body and the vocal folds begin to malfunction in a crackly deep tone. The effect is not healthy if used constantly, can be annoying to many and leaves the listener with a feeling there may be an underlying psychological message (maybe that you don't want to be there, or that you simply don't care). Remember: the word 'inspire' is derived from the verb to 'breathe'; with the lack of air inherent in vocal fry, the speaker is unable to inspire anyone.

While I was speaking with the assistant, I wondered: does she not realise that speaking in this way for a large part of her day is physically and psychologically disturbing? I believe, as did the Romans, that 'voice is a choice'—and if 'voice is a choice', why would you choose that one?

In our modern times you can simply turn on the TV and watch Australian politicians stumble for words, struggling against a broken flow of air from their body and finishing sentences with a weak cadence. This leads us to one inevitable outcome—a perceived lack of trust and respect and, therefore, the loss of gravitas.

I hear about similar experiences through my clients all the time. For example, when one of my clients, Gill, rang for help, I could hear the gasping of air as she grabbed a quick breath in between words. She was experiencing a common phenomenon where the throat closes with tension, and as the throat closes, the air is forced through a tighter passage, leading to an audible wheezing sound.

This created an annoying audible component to her voice. Firstly, it is unhealthy, but it can also be frightening to those around us as it unconsciously causes us to imagine danger, by anticipating fear from the speaker.

Another of my clients, Jane, got in touch to work on her voice and presence. When speaking with her you can hear her voice shoot upwards in pitch at the end of almost every sentence. This is something a lot of people do in certain Australian regions, including North Queensland. In normal conversation, this way of speaking (called 'uptalk') is employed to sound easy-going, friendly and non-threatening. However, in a business presentation it turns every sentence into a question and undermines the speaker's credibility and gravitas.

Jack is told he speaks too fast. He can feel how fast he speaks, just as he can feel his heart race, his fingers shake and his perspiration increase. So he thinks the solution is to speak more slowly. But as he learns through learning about the voice, the solution is actually to stand up straight and breathe between sentences.

Aneeta can be speaking in a perfectly normal tone to an individual, but as soon as she walks in front of the group her voice pitch shoots up into the stratosphere. This is a result of body tension and a visual learning preference, but people just tell her she 'lacks gravitas'. So to respond, she tries to speak in a lower pitch. But she can only manage to retain that for about five seconds and then she returns to the same high pitch. The solution is in the body and breath, not in attempting to consciously alter her pitch.

Anton keeps 'shooting his head off his body' every time he makes a sound. This is where the body stays static, but as one speaks, the head shoots forwards horizontally (in singing I have heard people describe this as the chook, as it looks like a chicken strutting). It makes him look distorted and strangles his sound. Those around him just say 'Well, that's just Anton.' But it isn't Anton at all. It's Anton with a very unhealthy habitual pattern.

I could go on, but I think you will already recognise one or more of these examples, either in yourself or in someone that you know. They're around us every day.

Contemporary Vocal Models

For those with no psychological or physical limitations and who just want to sound a little better when they speak, it's natural that they would look for answers in the world of modern voice studies. And just as we turn to body language as our guide to the body, we turn to nonverbal studies for voice.

While the juxtaposition of 'voice' and 'nonverbal' at first seems counterintuitive, in this case, one is a part of the other. Broadly, nonverbal communication refers to communication by means other than the words themselves. In this chapter, we aren't talking about voice in terms of the words we're saying, but voice in terms of its use as an instrument—the sound, pitch, volume and more that create an individual's unique vocal production. In this way, 'voice' is in fact an element of nonverbal studies. Modern nonverbal studies do deal with voice but focus primarily on a one-way (or linear) model of communication that considers content to be transmitted between the 'sender', using the medium of voice, to the 'listener' (Chapter 2 explores this model of communication in more detail).

As I worked in this field over the years, I found (mostly within the margins of nonverbal studies) divisions within divisions, a theory of relationships that was consciously egotistic, with a lack of concern for authenticity of expression and an undermined concern for voice—relegating voice to the position of poor cousin to the family of research on body language (and that is being polite!).

Contemporary nonverbal studies have consistently failed to provide tangible, practical skills to voice users. Despite the claim of a huge proportion of communication being voice-focused, voice has always been the poor cousin. It reminds me of the evolution of rhetoric, diminished from its five canons to the two canons of arrangement and style in the modern age, negating invention, memory and delivery (Chapter 1 explores this oversimplification of the canons of rhetoric in more detail).

The surprising anomaly here is that nonverbal research attributes a large proportion of the communication function to voice. Although research varies,[22] some figures suggest that nonverbal factors account for as much as 93 per cent of the total impact of a message, of which voice is up to 40 per cent.[23] Other research suggests nonverbal factors account for 70 per cent of communication.[24] But whether it's 93 per cent or 70 per cent or some other percentage, the fact is that voice matters in our communications.

It is interesting, therefore, given this attributed importance, to note the voice's almost complete absence within the study of communication. One text, which is used as a nonverbal studies reference in at least one Australian university, contains only 18 pages (from a total of 400) devoted to voice.[25] That's a mere 4.5 per cent of the book!

Similarly, in another textbook that's in use at an NSW university, six lines on a single page of the 577-page book relate to voice.[26] In Granvill N Toogood's famed nonverbal communication book, *The Articulate Executive*, just as it barely touches on delivery, of the 198 pages, I could find only one page devoted to 'sound'.[27] This surprising near-omission made me question how anyone could hope to become the next 'articulate executive', without any focus on voice.

The exclusion of voice is puzzling, given its apparent importance. How can it be relegated to almost total irrelevance? The answer perhaps lies in the lack of applicable vocal knowledge gained from a field focused on the perception of voice and lacking any understanding of vocal development.

Perceptions of the voice

In the context of corporate or work organisations, we have certain perceptions of the voice, which could include attractiveness, credibility, competence, confidence and dominance. These are very interesting and a useful tool for analysis (as opposed to 'change') as our perception impacts our ability to trust in what we hear:

- **Attractiveness.** An attractive voice is generally considered to be 'more articulate, lower in pitch, higher in pitch range, low in squeakiness, non-monotonous, appropriately loud and resonant'.[28] Expert researcher on the theory of attractiveness, Diane S Berry, further explains: 'People with attractive voices are then considered to have more power, competence, warmth and honesty. On the other hand, people with babyish voices are usually perceived to be less powerful and less competent but warmer and more honest than people with mature, sounding voices'.[29]

- **Credibility.** Generally, the standard dialect of an area tends to enhance a speaker's credibility in formal settings, whereas ethnic and in-group dialects are preferable in informal contexts, such as at home or in bars.[30] Also, when the degree of accent is an important consideration for stereotyping and categorising people, the more intense the accent, the more negative the impact on credibility, so much so that consistently mispronounced words may impair a speaker's credibility and communicative effectiveness.[31] Think for instance of someone with a strong Irish accent giving a presentation about finance. Some may find this difference to an Australian accent undermines credibility, whereas when we meet them in the pub in the evening, they are the toast of the town.

- **Competence.** Audiences tend to believe that a person is more competent as their rate of speech increases,[32] although there is a point at which the speaking rate becomes so fast that any positive effect becomes negative. The example of my client Jack, who has been told he speaks too quickly, is applicable here as well. Rather than being a positive, the speed of his speech was just too much, and distracted from his gravitas.

- **Confidence.** The confident voice is considered to be one that has substantial (but not excessive) volume, utilises a rapid speaking rate and is both expressive and fluent. Stuttering, incomplete sentences, overuse of 'ah' or other 'filler' words, or slips of the tongue are often strongly associated with high levels of anxiety.[33]

- **Dominance.** Dominant and powerful individuals are believed to speak with a voice that is flowing and smooth (free from 'hesitation and hedges'). On the other hand, when an individual speaks in a halting style, they are perceived as being a submissive and low-power person.[34]

Stereotypes, authenticity and the 'fake it to make it' brigade

The perceptions of voice covered in the preceding section (which are so ingrained they near the realm of stereotype) are the most frequent findings in contemporary studies on the relationship between voice and perceptions. In fact, studies show that even in courts of law, judges will assign a personality trait to a particular voice style, even if the person's actual personality is different.[35]

These perceptions help us to understand one key train of thought about authenticity and voice: that the accuracy of the conclusions an audience reaches about a speaker don't matter that much at all. What matters is *how* the speaker is perceived.[36]

In modern training, public speakers are told to, work on presentation manners

that lead audiences to draw desired or undesired inference about them which, whether accurate or not, affect the continuation and effectiveness of the communication situation. If a speaker is perceived as effeminate, arrogant, unscrupulous, or incompetent because of vocal cues ... his actual personality and credibility may be superfluous'.[37]

This has led modern leaders to join the 'fake it to make it' brigade—adopting 'voice' traits that they believe will showcase how they want to be perceived, rather than utilising their own characteristics to showcase their personalities and expertise. This is part of where our understanding of voice has gone wrong.

Pitch, pace and volume

One of the fascinations for me is when clients come to me worrying about their own voice and wondering how they might change it for the better. The first things they always want to address are pitch, pace and volume. They believe this is where the changes should be made.

When it comes to change in everyday speech, however, it's almost impossible to consciously control your pitch, pace and volume without sounding enormously manufactured. This was the downfall of the school of elocution and remains a misguided platform for change today.

Where did we go wrong?

There are several challenges with our current approach to the study of voice and nonverbal communication. The first is that there is a focus on perception (a focus that leads to self-consciousness) that has driven us towards the desire to improve how we are perceived, rather than train our voices to better communicate. And because we have been taught that voice is simply the combination of the three areas of pitch, pace and volume, then we think we need to change these three elements. Unfortunately, this line of thinking has led to frustration because it simply doesn't work. Instead, this focus on the wrong things leads to unnatural modes of speech, when we find ourselves coming across as inauthentic and fake in our communications. When we approach others to solve this new problem, we're often left with the advice to just 'be yourself'. Yet, if we felt we could just be ourselves, we wouldn't be in this position in the first place!

Secondly, if we believe there are people 'faking it to make it' in terms of voice and speech, then we start to worry that we are being deceived by others who are communicating with us. The most common question I am asked is, 'How do you spot a liar?' The thing is most people lie each day; some say up to 15 little lies a day. The challenge we need to meet is recognising that the people we are communicating with are real people, with essentially good intentions, who are simply doing their best and trying to be heard. The more authentic we can make our communications, the better we are able to communicate in a way that engenders trust and confidence.

New ways of looking at pace, pitch and volume

Research shows that a suitable rate of speech (demonstrating competence) is 110 to 150 words per minute.[38] Other research shows that an increased rate of speech shows intelligence, as well as confidence, objectivity and superior knowledge.[39]

Rate of speech is actually a very personal thing, and asking yourself to speak more slowly is not always the answer. Usually that kind of personal instruction lasts literally only seconds! Being in control of your rate of speech is a special art few can manage.

The role of the breath

If you receive feedback that you 'speak too fast', I would suggest that this is merely a perception. It may seem at first to be a rate of speech issue, but it is far more likely to be about the breath. When we breathe very high in our upper body, we tend to grab tiny amounts of air quickly between sentences. And it is that lack of a gap that brings people to the assumption that you are speaking too quickly.

The solution therefore is not to work on your pace of speech (as is often proposed, but is difficult to manage) but to work on the breaths between sentences. Each breath needs to be active low in the body and go deeper and last longer than a high-breath grab.

Patrica Frip, a well-known speaker and trainer in the United States, is someone who has devoted her life to speaking. Ms Frip's excellent advice is that: 'It is actually okay to speak fairly rapidly as long as you leave yourself room for pauses and silence. The faster you talk, the longer your pauses should be.'[40]

She suggests that as a speaker you need to give your audience time to digest what you've said. Her example is that if you ask the audience to 'consider the proposal in front of you', then you need to give them the time to do just that—to consider.[41] Your pauses allow them to do that.

In order to achieve these pauses, we need to focus on slowing down. Ms Frip also gives us a fantastic exercise to help us slow down. She says that when you're practising your speech, you should pause for one second at every comma, for two seconds at the end of every sentence and for three seconds after every paragraph. Then, she ends by asking us to breathe and smile, always good advice![42]

Reshaping the Paradigms and Models around Voice

Voice in the Western world has become a poor cousin when it comes to communication, and as a consequence we are adopting damaging and ugly sounds that also undermine our message.

Behind this is a one-way model of communication that doesn't recognise three important things:

1. the mind-body-voice connection (explored earlier in this chapter in the section 'The Romans and Voice')

2. the two-way model of communication (refer to Chapter 2)

3. that voice is a kinaesthetic (a physical movement of the body) as well as auditory vehicle (a movement of sounds).

The one-way model in turn reinforces the perception that we lack authenticity and leads us to stall in our ability to transform our own voices.

Watch for emperors with no clothes

People who have a wonderful voice seem to think they know how to help you. These are the people who tell you to slow down, lower your pitch or get rid of fillers like 'um'. I like to think of them as 'emperors with no clothes'.

While we can analyse how others hear us speak, and consider their reports on our pitch, pace and volume, we shouldn't be compelled to take their feedback as a guide for personal change. *Breath* is the basis for change. Real change to the voice happens from within, not from without.

Developing the voice

When it comes to developing the voice, one of my clients, Chris, bemoaned how she simply couldn't hear what she was doing. 'I just can't hear it!' she repeated *ad nauseam*. While to her it all seemed hopeless, I knew she could. She had just bought into the belief that her voice has a life of its own and that she was not in control.

For Chris, and for all of us, our funny old unconscious mind can fool us into not believing in ourselves and lead us to protect our defence patterns at all costs! And when Chris and I began working together, it didn't take more than five minutes before, bingo, suddenly she COULD hear it and we were on our way towards change.

It's because of the years of neglect in this field that I find myself wrestling with clients who can't 'hear' themselves and who tell me that changing their patterns doesn't 'feel natural'. This is when I jump in to say that we are talking about 'habitual' skills, not 'natural' functions at all.

Other clients claim to be 'introverts', which they feel excuses them from altering their speaking pattern. In another last-ditch, desperate attempt to hang onto old patterns, I am regularly regaled by clients with the excuse that they are 'left handed'. That's when I know the excuses have hit rock bottom (the left hand has no impact on the voice whatsoever!).

My Viennese mentor would laugh until she cried if she heard these excuses, and I dread to think how the ancients would respond.

But just as with Chris, change begins in as little as five minutes. That's all it takes. You just need to be willing to take the five minutes.

Developing your voice in practice

Unlike the way we've been taught by contemporary studies, we do have the ability to develop our natural voice in a way that is both authentic to ourselves and our natural sounds and congruent to the kind of leader that we want to be. This isn't a 'fake it to make it' approach. Instead, it's about developing 'good voice skills' that can lead to more gravitas. And just as we focus on becoming better leaders by learning leadership skills, we can become a leader with more gravitas by learning voice skills.

While we can develop our voice skills in a wide range of ways, they all come down to five essential areas.

1. **Instrument.** In practice, before you can start developing your voice, it's essential to ensure you have a healthy instrument—in other words, a voice that is undamaged. In almost every case, this will be true as it is unusual to be born with a voice that is not in good condition (though I have seen occasions where the voice has been destroyed by vocal abuse, this is rare).

2. **Posture.** Next you must set up your instrument, which is your body. Like a violin, you cannot play it if it is still in the case. Similarly, you cannot play your instrument, the voice, if the body and neck are folded over. This comes down to your posture. Stand up straight, have your head balanced on your body and keep your neck flexible.

3. **Breath.** Now, check that your vehicle of sound, your breath, is flowing correctly. This means the stomach goes in when

the breath is moving out of the body and vice versa for the breath in. Ensure your arms remain loose and not clenched against your sides, so that your breath can flow smoothly through your body.

4. **Blockages.** In my book *Resonate* I identify and discuss seven blockages to sound and provide techniques to overcome them.[43] You may find it helpful to explore these further.

5. **Practice.** These techniques allow you to practise initiating sound until you no longer habituate a stress pattern. Eventually, you can practise until you not only get it right, but can't get it wrong.

Summary

Learning from the ancients, we can adopt some main principles with regards to voice:

1.   Each person is born with a perfect vocal instrument.

2.   Voice gives you an enormous range and flexibility of sound.

3.   There are no bad sounds, just the perception of bad sounds.

4.   Voice is released, not taught.

5.   The mind is reflected in voice through the mind-voice-body connection.

We've also learned that developing the voice involves:

1.   ensuring you have a healthy instrument (the voice)

2.   having good posture

3.   managing your breath

4.   understanding the effects of stress and knowing the techniques to overcome stress

5.   practising until the patterns become habitual.

Most importantly, we understand the role that voice plays in our nonverbal communications, and the important role that nonverbal communication plays in our speaking and delivery generally. To deliver well, with gravitas, we must be able to use the voice to our best advantage.

Chapter 6
Can Women Have Gravitas?

One of the questions that I'm asked the most in my work is: can women have gravitas? To this, I give a resounding yes! However, I still see crises of confidence in women when it comes to speaking and delivering that centre around the belief that they cannot, in fact, have gravitas. This must be remedied.

Much of the research around confidence is done in the workplace. Some of the most concerning statistics are reflected in a 2011 study by the Institute of Leadership & Management in the United Kingdom, where British women were asked how confident they feel in their professions. The overwhelming answer was 'not very', while, on the other hand, less than a third of their male colleagues reported self-doubt.[1]

Other disturbing research shows that men initiate salary negotiations four times as often as women[2] and that women report salary expectations between 3 and 32 per cent lower than those of men for the same jobs.[3]

The problem reaches murkier depths when we discover that men consistently overestimate their abilities, while women consistently underestimate theirs. In addition, Hewlett-Packard found women only applied for jobs when they were 100 per cent certain of the job requirements. Men applied with a 60 per cent degree of certainty.[4] This is known as the 'male hubris, female humility effect'[5] and, importantly (and sadly), it's demonstrative of the crisis of confidence that women are experiencing in the workplace.

It is also a worry to know that when women finally do reach positions of leadership, they continue to experience their voice being marginalised. Women remain in the minority in meetings, and they speak 75 per cent less than their male counterparts when outnumbered. But men will speak as they always do regardless of the makeup of the sexes within the room.[6]

Although the work I do is for everyone who struggles with public speaking, it is essential that we learn to bridge the gender gap. Applying the skills for confidence is a major motivator for this book and I urge women leaders and emerging leaders, and those in a position to support change, to use this book as a starting point to help them change these statistics. That is the only way that we're going to see confidence in women build.

Research contained in Sylvia Hewlett's book, *Executive Presence*, shows that 67 per cent of senior executives surveyed saw gravitas as the core characteristic of executive presence.[7] But despite the importance of gravitas for all leaders (and I'd argue for all people!), I continue to be asked whether gravitas is also suitable 'for women'. The question arises as to whether gravitas will make them appear arrogant or hinder them from meeting gendered expectations of 'being nice'.

The answer is that gravitas may even be more important for women than for men. And it does not, in any way, involve being, or appearing, arrogant and, therefore, has no inherent conflict with the ideals of 'niceness'.

While we may associate gravitas today with weight and seriousness, this was never the intention of the ancient Romans. In fact, the Romans often spoke of the balance between weight and levity, including the use of humour, humility and wit. We have lost these elements of gravitas over the years, but that doesn't mean they don't still apply — it just means that we've forgotten how important it is to include them. We've been so focused on the 'weightiness' of gravitas, that we've neglected just those things (humour, wit, humility and more!) that makes gravitas the leadership quality that we need in our modern era. It's time to rebalance our understanding of gravitas with these elements in women's favour.

The Romans and Gravitas for Women

It is true that in Rome, gravitas was seen as a virtue for men, while women, on the other hand, embraced *prudentia* or 'prudence', which encompassed foresight, wisdom and personal discretion. However, the reason for this difference was not about the ability of women to have gravitas but simply because, at the time, women were not part of the public sphere. And because of that, they were not expected to seek out or obtain gravitas.

This explains why only men become orators. In ancient Rome, women weren't included in the public arena anywhere. They played no role in politics or business dealings. They did not ride horses or run marathons. And in theatres, they played no role and, in fact, when women were in the audience they sat with the slaves, the lowest level of society.

In contrast, women play an equal role in society today (at least in theory, if not in practice, as we still have a large gender gap in many areas). They are present on the sporting fields, in races, in politics, in the theatre and certainly in business. And, likewise, today's women deserve a similar opportunity to own their place in communications that allows them to express themselves with gravitas.

For the Romans, gravitas was of the utmost importance. It was one of the three foundational virtues of ancient Rome, the other two being *dignitas* (dignity) and *pietas* (respect)—Chapter 1 breaks down the definition of gravitas and these foundational virtues in further detail. If we're looking to see whether gravitas can apply to women, we first need to look at the application of these virtues, and we can clearly see that there is no gender conflict here. In fact, dignity and respect are universal traits that do not require any specific chromosome.

Second, we need to review Aristotle's five canons of rhetoric (as outlined in Chapter 1). There is nothing in the first four canons—invention, arrangement, style or memory—that is better suited for the male mind or body than the female. Women can have expertise of knowledge as much as the next (male) person and arranging information, considering language and memorising the information seems universal.

Third, we consider the fifth canon, delivery, which is where the confusion about whether or not women can have gravitas seems to arise. It is during delivery that we need to incorporate the skills of body and voice, and it is also in the delivery of information that women and men have obvious differences.

Ingredients of Delivery

A mediocre speech supported by all the power of delivery will be more impressive than the best speech unaccompanied by such power.[8]

— Quintilian

To understand the gender norms around gravitas, let's consider the key ingredients of delivery—namely posture, eyes, voice, and gestures and movement.

Posture

With posture, the aim is to have a body in balance and upright. Any posture of arrogance, such as a head tilted backwards or a lifted upper chest, were not standards of good health or posturing—and no woman or man is better suited to adopt them. However, our modern society is one of visual judgement, on all people, but far more on women. Anecdotally, 'advice' from well-meaning colleagues and bosses has always been that a strong stance in women (for example, power poses on stage) would lead to negative emotional reactions by the audience to the women.[9] Yet, studies show this to be absolutely incorrect. Power posing works just as well for men as for women,[10] so good posture and a strong stance is equally applicable to both sexes.

Eye contact

Many believe that gravitas involves strong eye contact. This is correct, but it is vital that we aren't just robotically staring; that is, holding the eyes without blinking. To stare would be aggressive, and the key to softening the eyes is to have some movement. This may be through nodding, changing the shape of the face through smiling or, the most important aspect, blinking. So what is the blink rate? Well, research shows that 15 blinks per minute is optimal for the look of 'listening',[11] and although research varies between activities and thinking, the key message is that blinking is important. All of this can lead to very soft eye contact, and there is no need to fear aggressiveness as long as one knows how to make the best use of eye contact.

Looking at the differences between male and female eye contact and gazing behaviours, research shows that women are more likely to use eye contact to check in and bond with others. They're also more likely to lower their eyes in submission, having been taught (consciously or subconsciously) that this would be viewed as aggressive or dominating and is therefore unacceptable for the 'fairer' sex. On the other hand, men use eye contact to demonstrate their dominance and to show that they have the higher-ranking status. If gravitas was actually a form of dominance and aggression, perhaps men would be naturally better at the eye contact that could deliver gravitas. But as it is not, they are not, and women are just as likely to be able to use good eye contact for engaging their audience and leading with gravitas as are men.

Voice

With voice, there are distinct differences between men and women. A woman's vocal folds are half the size of a man's and, consequently, most women naturally speak at a pitch approximately one octave higher than men.

In fact, a female's pitch range generally falls somewhere between 160–300 Hz, while a male's voice can be 60–180 Hz.[12] That's a big difference...with barely an overlap.

The Romans, however, never focused on pitch, the area where men are perceived to have an advantage. Instead, they spoke clearly about how to *produce* the voice (through practice and training), which is applicable for all humans. They also spoke of emphasis, tone and pace and, again, nothing here negates women from meeting those ideals.

In terms of volume, it is true that male voices, coming from a larger instrument, can often be louder. But even in terms of carrying power, women's voices have an advantage in that higher pitches naturally travel further. It is my belief that women should be embracing the natural sounds of their voices, and that there is nothing in their voices that will prevent them from developing their own gravitas.

Of course, I understand that this is contentious, as for years experts have advised women to adopt the low, slow and loud voice of leadership—with international examples including Margaret Thatcher and Elizabeth Holmes, both of whom altered their voices to achieve that notion of power. However, recent research has shown that the perceived lower voice for leadership is no longer a barrier to women[13] as we are beginning to change that perception. And indeed, perception is all that it is.

Midam Kim from the University of Kansas School of Business, nominated for the Phillips and Nadkarni Award for Best Paper on Diversity and Cognition, has undertaken research that sheds new light on pitch perception.[14] She has examined how low voice pitch is known to be an auditory cue for leader dominance and is therefore preferred by followers in various fields, mostly those with male leaders. But Kim's research shows that gender moderates this relationship, with the pitch effect becoming weaker when leaders are female. In other words, when the leader is female, a low pitch becomes less important.

Gesture and movement

Next are the areas of gesture and movement. These are areas where I believe women can strongly lead the way.

Unfortunately the elements of movement and gesture have almost completely disappeared from current presentations. Today the audience tends to sit at tables, leaving the most powerful spatial position in the room to the PowerPoint slides, while we, as speakers, stand robotically behind lecterns in the weakest part of the room.

But gravitas requires movement and freedom—and just as the ancient Romans and Greeks used the full space around them, so must we. Women can lead the way by recognising that different areas have different psychological meanings, and that gestures free the body and bring it to life.

For instance, when one finds the central position at the front of the room, it is useful to take that space to begin a conversation or a presentation. However, as one moves to stories or asks for questions, it makes sense to move to the side, which has more of the flavour of a facilitator. These movements back and forth are not wandering as these spaces have psychological meaning, and as long as the movement is aligned with the presentation, it will enhance the content. This is like a dance, and there need be nothing necessarily masculine about it.

Individuality and artful expression

The ancient Romans and Greeks valued individuality. Orators were renowned for the individual approaches they brought to their speeches, and critiqued by other orators and scholars of the time for their good and their bad techniques and styles. There was no one style required for an oration to be powerful, meaningful and impactful. The oration itself was instead an art, formed by the unique speaker's 'brush'.

As Quintilian observed:

> One remark must, however, be added, namely that as the great object to be regarded in speaking is decorum, different manners often become different speakers, and for such variety there is a secret and inexplicable cause. Though it is truly said that our great triumph is that what we should be becoming, this, as it cannot be accomplished without art, can still not be wholly communicated by art.[15]

There is no question in my mind that should Cicero or Quintilian be here today, they would be advocating for women just as they did for men.

The Future of Leadership Is Women

Everyone wins when there are more women in leadership positions. Research shows that organisations with more women on their boards outperform those without significantly.[16] Organisations that have a greater gender diversity in their senior leadership are more profitable. In fact, women in key leadership roles added a market value of between $52 million and $70 million per year for the average organisation.[17]

Women should not be held back by old-fashioned thinking that gravitas requires any masculine qualities. Being soft, flexible, gentle, speaking with a feminine sound—none of these are limitations of gravitas, despite what we've been taught by society and by previous leaders. In fact, the world is now primed for leaders who embrace their own unique nature—feminine or not—to bring the world an individual perspective, expertise and talent, all while delivering strong leadership backed by true gravitas.

Summary

It seems that not only is gravitas relevant for women, but that women can work with the rules of gravitas and rebuild a new way to establish their presence and influence moving forward. The future will be equally female led, strong and, yet, soft and flexible, with wit and humour.

Chapter 7
A Modern World

Of Aristotle's five canons of rhetoric, introduced in Chapter 1, we have so far only explored delivery in detail. In this chapter, we turn to the remaining four canons—invention, arrangement, memory and style—to explore how these important elements of communication work in our modern world, and how they contribute to gravitas.

Ask yourself, where have you been offered a course in the skills of rhetoric? Many of the programmes available, at least in Australia, exist in the schools of journalism and focus on the court or political system. And yet the advice of the ancient Greeks and Romans is no less relevant to us all today... and relevant to all people who need to communicate better.

Yes, we need some adjustment to account for modern thinking. But the ancients' way of viewing communication, with their focus on delivery (covered in Chapters 3, 4 and 5), the canons of invention, arrangement, memory and style, as well as persuasive communication that exists outside of spoken language itself (known as non-discursive rhetoric), forms a fabulous basis for our own communication.

And though the biggest leap in better communications will come from delivery, these other elements form part of the backbone of what we need to do in our modern area to achieve the gravitas we're striving for. I'd like to show you how.

Invention

It is from these and other authors worthy of our study that we must draw our stock of words, the variety of our figures and our methods of composition, while we must form our minds on the model of every excellence. For there can be no doubt that in art no small portion of our task lies in imitation, since, although invention came first and is all-important, it is expedient to imitate whatever has been invented with success.[1]

—Quintilian

The first of the five canons of rhetoric is invention. This is the stage where the speaker will brainstorm and conceptualise the main themes of their communications, do any research and make a general plan. It is really the thinking and planning stage, more than anything else.

When it comes to the 'invention' of the speech or presentation, the audience is still of the utmost importance. It is here that we begin to embrace the two-way communication model of Rome, because we need to select a topic that matters to the audience, and research sources and stories that will appeal to them specifically. If you are speaking about something the audience doesn't care about all that much, it won't matter how effectively the invention stage prepares you, or how much you invest into any of the other canons of rhetoric. Your audience simply won't care enough to listen.

As discussed in Chapter 1, you can research your subject and develop your concept using the canon of invention by:

- reading good books

- reading a lot of books

- reading dictionaries

- reading aloud to yourself

- using your expertise daily so it remains up-to-date and relevant.

Today, of course, we have to also factor in the enormous amounts of research available on the internet. The challenge here is to make sure you are not distracted by material that is not relevant to your subject.

In modern terms, things haven't changed all that much in the canon of invention. However, we do have to be careful not to rely on our expertise to the point that it becomes stale or outdated, or to the point that we fail to back it up with the work we need to do to become true experts. This expertise needs to be at your fingertips so you can harness it when it comes to brain storming and mind mapping your speeches, presentations and other communications.

The goal is, as Quintilian asks:

How can we conceive of any real eloquence at all proceeding from a man who is ignorant of all that is best in the world?[2]

Arrangement

It is through the Arrangement that we set in order the topics we have invented so that there may be a definite place for each in the delivery.[3]

It is the area of 'arrangement' that took up so much space in the writing of Aristotle and has been the focus for so many people since the days of ancient Greece, including in our schools of rhetoric today in contemporary universities. And while Aristotle's views on arrangement are magnificent, their focus on the courts and politics is generally not relevant to modern communicators in everyday interactions.

In our work today, we are looking to utilise practical, easily applicable and immediately useful skills. If I were to return to the language of the ancients—and use terms such as *enthymeme* (an argument in which one premise is not explicitly stated), stasis (the 'stand') or exordium (the 'opening')—I might lose everyone around me.

Instead it is a matter of moulding the ancients' knowledge into contemporary frameworks that are easily applicable, but still remain true to the elements of rhetoric. We can learn much from the way the ancients arranged an argument and the rule of three that is used as a tool to present memorable ideas, while adopting a clean, psychologically sound structure. As Quintilian notes, 'The gift of arrangement is to oratory what generalship is to war.'[4]

The ancients spoke of arranging an 'argument' in the following manner:

- exordium—the introduction

- narratio—where facts are laid out

- partitio—outlines what will follow

- propositio—the message

- confirmatio—arguments in favour of the propositio

- refutatio—arguments that could be brought against the propositio

- peroratio—conclusions.

Today, our needs, and hence our arrangements, are slightly different. We are not arguing cases in courts of law where we need specific arguments that are brought against the propositions.

However, it is the subject of another book to outline the contemporary models in full. Suffice to say that one needs a minimum set of arrangements that generally include the elements of 'argument' (exordium, narratio, partitio, propositio, confirmatio, refutatio and peroratio) for all of the following types of communications:

- answering a question simply

- answering a question with no elaboration

- breaking bad news

- giving a presentation

- answering difficult emotional questions (those that elicit emotion from the questioner or that raise emotion within oneself)

- giving feedback to change behaviour

- ending a hostile engagement.

Let's look at three of these as examples of how we might consider arrangement in our modern times:

- answering a simple question

- giving a presentation

- answering difficult emotional questions (those that elicit emotion from the questioner or that raise emotion within oneself).

Answering a simple question

Answering a simple question can still lead to a rambling response, so it may be useful to adopt the adage:

Omne trium perfectum

This simply means 'Everything in three is perfect' in Latin.

In Kabbalah philosophy, the number three signifies harmony; to the Chinese, the number three is considered lucky; while in Christian lore, the number three represents wholeness, completeness and perfection.[5] Some say this phrase is said to have been conceived by Confucius in 500 BC, but in its Latin form the rule of three was very much at play in the time of ancient Rome and Greece.

The rhythm of three can be read and heard all around us in such triptychs as:

- God the Father, God the son, God the Holy ghost

- the past, the present and the future

- 3 little pigs, 3 blind mice, 3 little bears.

Working with this pattern, it may be useful to divide the answer to a question into three sections. A statement begins and ends the answer, and three backup points form the middle.

In my experience, I would take the notion of three even further. I would attempt to include in this statement the idea of three words, which also embraces the rhythm of three, such as:

- it's absolutely fascinating

- the answer is simple

- it's actually complicated.

In addition, the use of a link phrase between the first statement and the three backup points may be useful; for instance:

- and why I say that is ...

- and explaining that ...

- what I mean by that is ...

This pattern can be used for media interviews, job interviews, podcasts or panel discussions. In fact, the applications are endless.

Consider a job interview, where you are asked 'Why are you interested in this role?' Following the rule of three, your answer may be:

Statement: 'It's a perfect fit'
Link phrase: 'and I say that because'

1 Statement

2 Backup
1.
2.
3.

3 Statement

Three backup points:

    1.   'I have the skills,'

    2.   'the experience and'

    3.   'a passion to make a change.'

Statement: 'So I think the fit is perfect.'

The discipline of this structure not only sounds professional but gives you a framework to work with that can minimise stress. Nothing inspires confidence more than knowing where you are going! In fact, using this technique can work wonders for alleviating chronic 'ums' because the mind stops wondering where it is going next.

Giving a presentation

The pattern of three is also in play in the arrangement of a presentation. Consider these three stages.

In the first section, *tell 'em what you are going to tell 'em*, you can again divide the section into three.

Following the rule of three, my arrangement again breaks each section into three discrete parts. The second step, the message, may be best advised to follow the discipline of being three words. For instance, there are many famous messages that follow this advice. Some are:

- Stop the boats.

- It is time.

- We need you.

1 Tell 'em **what you are going to** tell 'em

2 Tell 'em

3 Tell 'em **what you told** 'em

One critical point to note is that the message (the propositio) is an expression of what the audience will do, think or buy as a consequence of your presentation.

I would, therefore, suggest the absence of words such as 'tell' or 'talk', which create a disconnection between you and the audience, representing only what you are going to do, *not* what they are going to experience.

For example, one might say:

'Today I am going to tell you about the results of our project.'

Instead, I suggest:

'Today we will review the results of our project.'

I also note that there is no point here that requires you to let the audience know how happy you are to be there. I suggest they really don't care. Instead, by focusing on how you speak to your audience, you will naturally begin to build the rapport that you need to create connection between you and your audience.

The agenda (the partitio) is also suggested to be divided into three and be considered as three points that support the message (the propositio).

For example, an agenda outline might cover:

- The past, the present and the future.

- The impetus to begin this project, what we did and the results we found.

- Results, prioritisation, next steps.

Suffice it to say, the *tell 'em* section of your presentation is your content. This is your expertise and something you are likely already doing well. So often, we simply give the content and completely ignore the setup (*tell 'em what you are going to tell 'em)* and close (*tell 'em what you told 'em*), which actually carry equal weight—not in the amount of time they take up, but in the value they give. I have, therefore, focused on those forgotten sections.

Having completed the *tell 'em* part of the modern arrangement, the *tell 'em what you told 'em* is simply a reverse image of the *tell 'em what you are going to tell 'em*. It finishes with a 'next action' for the listeners.

For example, the opening of a presentation may proceed as follows:

Structure		Content
Introduction	Who	What an amazing turnout this evening with so many people taking the time to travel here for our meeting at the community centre! There are some here I know well and some new faces, so for those who do not know me, my name is Joan and I was recently elected as the president of our association.
	Time	Over this last session before our tea-break this evening
	Topic	we will look at what the next year holds
	Message	and believe me, it will be exciting!
	Agenda	So, let's run through: • the past projects over the last year • our new proposed projects and • our plan to implement those projects over the next twelve months.

This is in no way an expansive explanation, as that requires another book. It is, however, an example of the way you can arrange a presentation. This is not something that comes off the top of the head. There are

Tell 'em **what you are going to** tell 'em	Rapport building	Who Time Topic
	Message	Message
	Agenda	1. 2. 3.

elements of structure that can be placed in a table and a separate column can be used to add appropriate words. Why recreate the wheel over and over. It can be more like colouring in squares, incorporating the rule of three and focusing on the delivery of material for influence.

This may sound prescriptive, but it's not. Like music, a composition follows structure and then blossoms. Creativity is born within boundaries and flourishes.

Answering difficult emotional questions

To understand another way that we can work with arrangement in our modern world, we can look at the framework for handling difficult situations—using a simpler, quicker arrangement that allows us to break the arrangement (process) down into words, gestures, posture and voice.

It may be simple, but there are several steps that lead to the final product, and you will see how it all comes together beautifully by the end of the process.

To begin, let's define the context. Here we are dealing with a difficult situation where either the emotion of the person you are interacting with is raised or your own emotion is raised. The minute this happens, we understand that we've triggered the need for the situation to be handled with special care and attention.

Let's consider this example.

Sanjay, the head of IT at his company, attends a board meeting. He has approached the board, who have little understanding of technology, and given a presentation, which culminated in him asking for a large sum of money to implement a major IT project. After his presentation, Sanjay is asked some questions from the board, and one in particular from a member who is worried about the lack of a guaranteed outcome. He wants to answer this question well—and how he responds is a part of the arrangement.

As is the case with all skills, we tend to have one pattern we use constantly when responding to questions—out on the streets, in the office, in our homes—a one-step process, which is to simply 'answer' the question.

Using this process, Sanjay may reply to the board member directly and simply state: 'The project is essential to the future of the organisation.' This is the simple, one-step answer to the question. While it provides a response, it doesn't really give the questioner much confidence in Sanjay or his project. We can do better. What are the options?

While the one-step answer is the most common pattern, other alternatives include asking more questions or associating blame with the other person. But if I were to ask, 'How are these methods working for you?', most people will say, 'Poorly!'

A better alternative is to follow the guidance of rhetoric—and the learnings of ancient Rome—and utilise a three-step framework. Remembering the rule of three, this process involves a response to the question that factors in three elements:

1. Acknowledge

2. Reflect

3. Answer

1 Acknowledge > 2 Reflect > 3 Answer

The three-step framework for arranging a response

This three-step framework was shared with me many years ago by colleague and psychologist Sharon Burrows, and has been tried and tested over decades by my clients in national and global engagements with astounding success. When we're referring to the second canon of rhetoric, this is our modern understanding of 'arrangement'.

ACKNOWLEDGE

Arrangement is simply putting our ideas into a logical and organised fashion. In the modern era, using this three-step process as a framework to manage a difficult question or situation within our presentations, the first step is to 'acknowledge'.

Acknowledging allows us to recognise there is a difficult situation and begin to work on finding an effective way to handle that difficulty. I find this place to start to be more like a martial arts warrior's approach to 'go with' the problem rather than go against it. Think of Jackie Chan in the movies, where with his first move he cleverly mirrors the movement of his opponent, matching his energy with the energy of the attacker, rather than hitting them head on with opposing forces.

As a Master Practitioner in neuro-linguistic programming (NLP), I recognise the idea that if an individual can understand how another person thinks (and therefore acts), they may be able to learn this way of thinking (and acting) as well. So, this acknowledgement aspect of the response is when you relive an experience, you put yourself in their shoes and you have all the feelings, as opposed to when you are disassociated and you observe only yourself. But another way to describe it—and perhaps more clearly—is to say that we are empathising with the other person.

For Sanjay, this would mean taking steps to recognise the concerns of the board member about not being able to guarantee any concrete outcomes. Using NLP he could place himself in the board's shoes, considering how they think about the situation and how this would impact their actions, and be able to craft his own communications around that understanding.

Furthermore, during the acknowledgement phase, there are words that are good to say and words that are best avoided. Being a phase of association and empathising, it is best to avoid the two words 'I' and 'understand'.

The first word, 'I', goes against the concept of empathising and makes the response one of 'sympathising', where we relate the situation to ourselves—which is not required at this stage.

To use the word 'understand' implies that you do know the situation and have had the same experience or emotional response the other person has experienced. Often this is not the case and can raise feelings of anger from others.

For example, imagine Sanjay speaking to the board about the need to spend copious amounts of the company's funds on a project that is considered to be high risk. To greet a board member's emotional response about the possibility of financial loss with the words 'I understand' would be a poor choice of words that could land Sanjay in a long, continued argument. The fact is, Sanjay really doesn't understand because from his perspective the risk isn't high at all. While this is a mistake most people make, the words 'I' and 'understand' turn the response to one that is sympathetic, not empathetic and will not engender a positive feeling.

More helpful words that are recommended for the acknowledgement step include:

1.   It's or That's...

2.   Thank you...

3.   I'm sorry...

For example, Sanjay might start by saying, 'That's a good point' or 'Thank you for sharing your perspective' or 'I'm sorry you see it that way.'

It is important to recognise here that you have a choice in how you respond, which helps you avoid the situation where you might find yourself stuck repeating 'That's a good question' *ad nauseam*. Instead, you now have a range of options so that you sound fresh every time.

REFLECT

The second step is to reflect. This means that you are listening to the other person, taking in the essence of their communication. You are thinking not just about what has been *said*, but what has been *meant*, and reflecting this meaning back to them.

One thing we need to recognise is that a listener's perspective changes once emotions are being raised. (Yes, even yours.) An apt metaphor is how when we fall asleep, we lose our sense of smell.[6] In the same way, when our emotions are raised, a listener cannot hear your answer or properly understand and reflect it back until they know you have heard their issue.

It is obvious when this stage has been ignored. In fact, ignoring this phenomenon leads facilitators and speakers to re-answer the same question over and over. However, when they hear the same emotional issue being raised multiple times, they need to stop and reconsider whether they have really reflected the concerns of those people.

Reflection is a critical step in the process of arrangement for two other reasons. One is that reflection ensures you do comprehend the issue at hand so that you can properly deal with it. Another is that it also buys you time to give the right answer.

Often we settle for reflecting the content of what is said, but what about the unspoken elements—the nonverbal communications (a focus of much of the thought here in this book)? These are part of the communication process, and they need to be reflected as well.

So, there are two parts to the practice of reflection:

- emotion

- content.

The emotion words need to actually be descriptions of emotions. For example:

- frustrated

- concerned

- worried.

The question now is the link. How do you get from the first step, acknowledgement, to the second, reflection?

A suitable link phrase may be to say:

So what you are saying is …

Others are to follow the three learning preferences for taking in information (seeing, hearing or feeling), with words such as:

1. looks like

2. sounds like

3. feels like.

Note the avoidance of the word 'I'. Avoid saying 'I see that…' or 'I hear that…' or 'I feel that…' because these could be alienating phrases.

ANSWER

The next step in the process is to put together your thoughtful and considered answer. You'll want to consider the words that will work most effectively to connect you with the listener (perhaps also considering any words that might antagonise the listener).

The link phrases between the reflection and the answer are endless. For instance, one may say:

- On the other hand…

- From my perspective…

- In answer to that…

We are moving here to bring the issue back to ourselves, but at the same time it is important not to negate the other person's issue by using the words 'but' or 'however'.

So let's return to our example of the upset board member. Following our process, Sanjay may say to the board member:

Thank you for your comments and I can see that it is frustrating to be spending vast amounts of money on a project when it is a fresh approach untested in the market. From the well-researched perspective of our team and in line with our goals and values as a market leader, I feel it is critical to make this investment to move forward at the leading edge of the market.

In one fell swoop, Sanjay has acknowledged, reflected and answered, and in doing so engaged in two-way communication that builds confidence, trust and, ultimately, gravitas.

	Words to say	Illegal words
1 **Acknowledge**	It's/That's... Thank you... I'm sorry...	I understand
	Looks like, Sounds like, feels like So what you're saying is	
2 **Reflect**	A. Emotion B. Content	
	On the other hand... From my perspective... In answer to that...	But However
3 **Answer**		

Delivery

Many may stop with this three-step framework, understanding that this creates a psychologically sound response. But, as we have learned, one of the most important steps is the next one—delivery.

Let's look at delivery in light of Sanjay's situation addressing the board. When Sanjay is addressing the board, he'll want to be thinking about his posture, his eyes, his gestures and his voice.

POSTURE

When delivering the answer to the board member's question, Sanjay needs to be aware of his posture. He needs to remember the aim of having his body balanced and upright, without his head being tilted too far backwards or forwards.

When receiving comments from the board members, Sanjay also needs to turn his whole body to face the person head on. During the reflection step, he remains facing the person. However, when answering, he should turn his body to the whole group.

EYES

Again, when delivering his answer, Sanjay should have strong but natural eye contact, remembering to blink (and not simply stare!). When receiving comments or dealing with tricky questions, Sanjay needs to have his eyes meeting the eyes of the person speaking for the acknowledgement and reflection steps. He then turns his eyes to the whole group when answering.

GESTURES

When organising your response to a difficult question, you also need to accompany it with gestures. Each stage of the process can have its own unique gestures that will be the nonverbal components of your overall communication. These gestures will also move you through each stage, acting as a memory technique (I will explore memory in more detail shortly).

When you're listening and responding to comments, there are some gestures that work well. Suggested gestures would be to take the rest position while listening, then when acknowledging to reach the arms out towards the person.

An interesting gesture that Sanjay may choose during the reflection step would be to take his hands to one side of his body and, as Sanjay is reflecting on the issue, to make a gesture away from the body to that side. Visually, this would look like Sanjay has two hands to one side of the body at waist level. Then, his two hands move to the other side of the body at waist level. This gesture has two purposes. One is to give the issue a place in space and the second is to make sure that place is outside of his own body.

It may also be useful to move the arms again, perhaps to the other side of the body, suggesting the idea that the challenge is on one side of the body and the solution on the other side.

VOICE

When considering the best use of voice during the difficult emotional question process, give some thought to mirroring the tone of the questioner at some point.

When you are implementing the three-step framework in order to manage tricky questions, there are three vocal suggestions you can try, one for each stage of the three-step framework:

*   **Acknowledge.** At the acknowledgement step, it could be useful to use the voice of caring, which involves breathing extra air into each word.

- **Reflect.** At the reflection step, it may be useful to take on the tone of the other person slightly, mirroring their voice with your own.

- **Answer.** As you approach the answer, this is where you tune in again to your most comfortable vocal tone.

These things are so hard to describe in writing and so much easier to explain in action! And this is, of course, a reason why much of this work was never written down. That, however, does not make it any less important.

Attempting to place this work in a chart, it may look as follows (see overleaf).

Of course, this is an awful lot to remember, particularly when you're in the midst of a presentation or speech. And that is why we also need to consider the fourth canon of memory.

Memory

Who isn't fascinated by the individual who has incredible feats of memory, remembering everyone's names, perhaps even the names of their kids or pets! We usually make the assumption that this person has incredible skills that are unattainable to all. However, if you enquire further you will discover that rather than an innate skill, this memory is actually the result of robust techniques and hours of rehearsal.

Showing once again that the ancients knew so much more about the canons of rhetoric, Quintilian tells us, 'If anyone asks me what is the one supreme method of memory, I shall reply, practice and industry.'[7]

	Words to say	Illegal words	Eyes	Gestures	Body	Voice
1 Acknowledge	It's/That's... Thank you... I'm sorry...	I understand	On person	Reaching towards them	Move forward	Breathy
2 Reflect	Looks like, Sounds like, feels like So what you're saying is A. Emotion B. Content	But However	On person	Arms move to one side		Imitating voice of the person with emotion
3 Answer	On the other hand... From my perspective... In answer to that...		Away from person	Arms move to opposite side	Turn body away	Your own vocal tone
	Words to say	Illegal words	Eyes	Gestures	Body	Voice

Research shows us that memory is more like a muscle than a shoe box.[8] With a shoe box, you have limited space. Once you have filled it, that's it. It will not contain any more. And if you try to cram more in, then the lid won't close. On the other hand, a muscle is built up over time, getting bigger and stronger the more you work with it. It grows in its capacity over time and with exercise.

Imagine a jogger attempting to jog after six months in a wheelchair recovering from an accident. It won't happen. But if the jogger starts with short walks, building up to longer walks, and then, ultimately, jogs, it's much more likely to be accomplished.

When it comes to memory, we need to continue to work it. It is fantastic that today we can find anything on the internet with just a few taps on our smartphone screens. But this ease of information gathering needs to be added to an already strong mind. If not, then like the tower of neck rings that stretch the neck of certain tribal women, your mind will become accustomed to the ease, and will weaken and fail, just like the necks of those women eventually become reliant on the support of the neck rings and would snap without them.

However, while an actor perfects the art and the skill to memorise a script and own it until it lives completely free in their mind, most of us cannot achieve that skill simply from presenting, even on a daily basis. In fact, the attempt to do so eventually becomes overbearing, leading to more stress and performance anxiety, and further undermining gravitas.

While coaching one of my global CEOs, he suddenly blurted out that he never understood how much people would be looking to him, nor that it was part of his job to present so much every day. 'I just can't remember it all,' he wailed.

'What technique are you using?' I asked, to which he replied that he was learning each presentation off by heart. Aha! That is the wrong game. And so we began to work together on the new game.

It is with the pulling together of the words that most will stop their concentration, but we are, of course, aware that we need to refocus our attention on the canon of delivery. And helpfully, the canon of delivery and the canon of memory go hand in hand.

So how do we use memory in our presentations? It often comes as a surprise to those that I work with that I don't recommend learning off by heart.

You see, the ancient Romans used techniques for memory that were focused on process, not rote word-for-word memorisation. And these are the techniques we can bring into our modern-day presentations.

There are similarities between the techniques. The point is that the ancient Romans and Greeks took this canon of rhetoric very seriously and actively worked to develop their memories—they never read their words from pieces of paper. The Roman orator Cicero also emphasised the importance of dividing information into small, digestible parts and connecting them in a logical sequence. This approach helped him with organising his thoughts and making them more memorable.

These memory techniques were highly regarded and widely practised in ancient Rome as effective methods for improving one's memory, and can still be applied today.

Remember, everyone's memory works differently, so it's important to find the techniques that work best for you. Experiment with different strategies and see which ones improve your memory the most. Here's how.

Have a framework

The first technique for memory is to have a framework. It is common when finding oneself in a difficult or stressful situation to struggle to think. But when you have a solid framework, you have created a simple way of having the information at your fingertips.

Speaking at a conference recently, health expert Michele Chevalley Hedge, globally accredited health and wellbeing speaker, said something that has stuck with me ever since. She said that eating the same thing for breakfast takes away an enormous decision-making load in a person's day. Similarly, having a framework for your presentation that is informed by research takes away the stress of reinventing the wheel every time.

Loci (the memory palace)

In *De Oratore*, Cicero tells the story of Simonides of Ceos, known as the inventor of the method of loci. According to Cicero, Simonides was invited to deliver a lyric poem at the house of a wealthy nobleman. A while later, a message was brought to Simonides and he was called outside urgently, but when he went out there was no one there. At that moment, the roof of the banquet hall where he had been delivering his poem fell in, crushing the nobleman and his guests.

The guests' families wanted to bury their loved ones but weren't able to identify them because of the violent way they'd been crushed. However, because of Simonides' memory device of loci, he could recall where each of the guests had been reclining at the table and was able to identify them for burial. While this was a good result for those grieving families, it was a great result for posterity as well because it led Simonides to conceptualise the idea of orderly arrangement as a memory aid—the method of loci.

Colloquially, the method of loci is often thought of as a 'memory palace'.[9] As a technique, you would think of your home, for example, and assign one item that you needed to remember to a room of the house. When you bring up the image of your home in your mind, you would be prompted to remember the various elements within those rooms. Studies show that this technique works just as well with new places — or even fictional places.[10]

For example, if you wanted to remember a series of items, you would visualise each item placed at various points along a familiar route. By mentally retracing your steps along that route, you could recall the items in the correct order. You could also do this by walking from room to room in the imaginary house.

When you are creating your presentation, you can use the device of loci to help you memorise the outline, which can then help you to move naturally through your presentation or speech without having to memorise anything word for word.

Architectural design

More recently, through NLP, I learned a twist on the technique of the memory palace. Rather than base your memory on an existing structure, you recreate your own house by anchoring items in the space around you through movement and gesture.

Using this technique, which I call 'architecturally designing' your presentation, you mentally place areas of information on different places around you on the ground and in the air. This spatial anchoring supports memory, but it has the added benefit of allowing movement that helps free the body.

Linking

Another memory technique is 'linking'. Linking is where you attach the item you want to memorise to something you already know — something that is not an object. It's more difficult to remember things in isolation than things that are interconnected with well-known ideas or concepts. Even crazy connections can work well, as long as a connection is there.

An example of linking is when you want to remember a historical date—say the Battle of Hastings, 14 October 1066. You might link that to your mum's birthday (14 October) and your anniversary (December 1966). You might imagine that you're in your wedding dress, eating cake with your mum at a huge Norman battle. It might be a little crazy, but that image will help you remember your date!

One form of linking—mnemonic techniques—involve associating new information with something you already know. This can be done by creating acronyms, visual images, rhymes or even placing things in alphabetical order or associating each letter with a word you already know, such as a name.

For example, if you need to remember the three reasons why it is important to make a change, you list out the three reasons. Perhaps you think they are:

1.   **Impetus:** The market is currently primed for the change.

2.   **People:** You have a great team of people.

3.   **Time:** The organisation is in a good position at the moment to make the change.

How will you remember those three points? Taking out the key words, you have impetus, people and time. Again this is not incredibly memorable, but you can change their order to be time, impetus and people, and taking the first letter of each of those words, you have the acronym TIP. So when it comes to remembering why we need to make change, all you have to remember is TIP and before you know it you are reeling off the information about it being the right time, with a great impetus to move and being implemented by the right people. Easy.

(Many memory champions and individuals interested in mnemonics utilise similar principles to the techniques shared in this chapter in their memorisation practices.)

Dissoi Logoi

The *Dissoi Logoi* is a (likely unfinished) manuscript that's sometimes attributed to Protagoras, the famous sophist (a sophist was a teacher of philosophy and rhetoric in ancient Greece associated more with scepticism and specious reasoning—a person who reasons with clever but false arguments). It's one of the sources for the sophist's approach to deliberation—which is to argue both sides of a question. The *Dissoi Logoi* argues that everything is relative—for example, what is bad for one is good for another, and what is just in one situation is unjust in another.

In the midst of its arguments for relativism, the writer also speaks to memory, stating that the first step is to 'focus your attention, your mind, making progress by this means, you will perceive more'. The second step is to then 'practice whatever you hear' and then what you have learned will remain in your memory 'as a connected whole'. The third step is that whenever you hear something new, 'connect it with what you know already'.[11]

This is excellent advice—focus, practice and connect—for remembering information generally, and specifically when developing a speech for delivery.

Gestures

Some do not recognise the benefit of gestures when it comes to helping us remember, yet they are a very useful technique.

Like a dancer, the gestures you include when arranging your answering techniques become a hint of the next 'movement' (or element) in your communication. Bodies have memory (we sometimes think of this as muscle memory), and when we create a choreographed set of gestures we build muscle memory that can help us remember the arrangement and content of our communications.

Style

The last canon to discuss is one of style. Style is the process of coming up with the actual words that you are going to use in your communication—whether that's a speech or a presentation or even an email. You can think of this as the 'writing stage'. I have placed style last in this discussion because, for us in the modern era, it is one of the least important canons; while style is important, we are not looking for poetry in business. We are simply looking for straightforward, clear speech that delivers the message well.

The elements of style in ancient Greece and Rome were correctness, clarity and appropriateness. For correctness, the words were to be in current usage. (Betwixt the words you might miss their meaning!) For clarity, jargon was shunned, and for appropriateness, the language used needed to be appropriate for the subject and the audience.

There were also three types of style—grand, middle and simple[12]—to which the elements mentioned above apply equally. Examples may be:

- **Grand:** Why do the donkeys of the valley refuse to carry their burden?

- **Middle:** Donkeys need to carry their weight.

- **Simple:** Get up donkey.

Style was individual and unique to the ancients. In Quintilian's time, 'silver Latin' (where ornate embellishment was favoured over precision and clarity) was the trendy style in oration.[13] But Quintilian himself recommended a return to simpler and clearer language during public speaking,[14] adopting Cicero's approach to oration.

In modern terms, your style in writing your content depends on both your audience and your own individual approach. For example, if you are a political candidate you might use humorous metaphors comparing parliament to a zoo. If you're a leader in a corporate organisation that creates toys, you might use playful and light language, particularly when speaking to your team or wholesalers.

The canon of style today isn't widely different from the canon the ancient Romans would have studied. But of course, the styles themselves will be far more modernised to account for modern thinking and modern audiences. The most important factor, as always, is to look to build connection with your audience. The more they feel connected to you, the more trust they'll have in you, and the more gravitas you'll have as a communicator overall.

Non-discursive Rhetoric

Non-discursive rhetoric is everything other than language or discourse (conversation). For instance, music, while it fulfils many emotional needs, is a non-discursive enterprise; it doesn't take place within language. In a similar way, you can think of non-discursive rhetoric as being like clothing—the visual stimuli that adds impact.

Ancient non-discursive rhetoric

In ancient Rome, the area immediately surrounding the Forum—in which most public speeches were delivered—was a space bounded by and composed of a vast assemblage of potent visual symbols of Roman religion, culture and history. Roman orators speaking in this space were surrounded by statues, temples, war trophies, altars, sacred sites, monuments, buildings and other physical objects possessing powerful emotional associations, symbolic meaning and identity.

During an oration, a speaker might point to a cult statue to allude to virtues associated with that deity, or to a public building to demonstrate the politics of that space. With the use of such non-discursive rhetoric, the words were simply not required.

The roofs and steps of temples in the area, such as the Temple of Jupiter Capitolinus, one of the most important temples in ancient Rome, were festooned with statues of gods and deities. With a simple pointing motion, a speaker could use these settings to emphasise, elaborate upon or even convey messages.

The senate house, known as the Curia Julia, where many orations were held, also contained its own communicative objects. There was *in situ* a statue of Victoria (the Roman goddess of victory) and paintings portraying an old man leaning on a stick, a two-horse chariot and a painting (brought over from Greece) of Nemea (the Naiad-nymph of the springs of the town of Nemea) clutching a palm branch and seated upon a lion. There was also a golden shield honouring the emperor Augustus and inscribed with the virtues of *clementia* (clemency), *justitia* (justice) and *pietas* (piety).

The objects were so numerous that nearly every historical or religious allusion in a speech could have been matched to a corresponding statue or monument. By a simple pointing motion, the speaker could use these settings to emphasise, elaborate upon or even convey messages.

Cicero explicitly equated a *contio*, Latin for a public assembly, with a stage that offered rich opportunities for manipulation and pretence.

A speech by Gaius Gracchus, as recorded by Cicero, demonstrates this use of gesture very well.[15]

In an attempt to emphasise his unhappy situation, Gaius repeatedly asked his audience, 'Where can I turn?' After each repetition, he suggested a destination that should have offered him refuge, such as the Capitol or his home, and then explained why he could not go there. Gracchus acted out his pleas by stretching out his arms and pointing towards each failed sanctuary in turn. So moving were his words and use of gestures that in the end even his enemies could not hold back their tears.[16]

Without these backdrops, it was unthinkable to present one's ideas, and Cicero, left in a bland environment, notes, 'My delivery is crippled by its surroundings.'[17]

The modern non-discursive world

When Trump made his entry for the New Jersey presentation, the entryway was draped strategically with the national flag. Symbols of nationalism were all around, and some say even his bizarre hairstyle is a wave to the average man. Yet many are unaware of the influential impact these symbols have in supporting Trump's message.

Of course, the Romans would believe (as do I!) that using this technique is good as long as the message is for good. However, if it is a message leading us in the wrong direction, it is not. The key is to be aware of the power of this technique and how it can be used.

In this book, we are focused on the human elements of gravitas, but one cannot negate the effect of what surrounds and supports us.

Today, we have lost many of the elements of the non-discursive world. We often present our ideas in bland rooms with white walls and no external reference. We enter a digital conversation with the image of an unmade bed behind us, seated against the backdrop of a blank white wall or even with the background fuzzed out completely, contemplating no awareness of the negative messages this might be sending.

But non-discursive communication is important. So here are three things you need in your background for a virtual meeting:

1. books

2. something alive (a plant)

3. something personal (a photo or award).

Alternatively, we have discovered digital backgrounds, and now we have entered the realm of PowerPoint, which in many cases has been misunderstood and used as an alternative to any rhetoric whatsoever.

Using PowerPoint is not the goal of this book, and suffice to say we are all aware that way too much information is often seen dumped on the screen with no thought to actually giving the listener any knowledge they can grasp. If you are looking for advice, then writers such as Nancy Duarte[18] have made major inroads in helping presenters use their PowerPoint presentations to tell their story.

The question I pose is: 'What is your backdrop, virtually and in real life?' And the challenge I put to you is that perhaps we have overcomplicated the whole thing. We need simple images with which the people around you can associate. Do you have paintings on your walls? Do your PowerPoint slides use images that speak a thousand words? Communication is not rocket science. You just have to think.

Summary

Implementing the elements introduced by the ancient Romans and Greeks—the rhetorical canons of invention, arrangement and memory, as well as non-discursive rhetoric—within our modern contexts and frameworks allows us to create better presentations, better speeches, better connection and better trust with our listeners. Most importantly, it allows us to build the opportunity for better delivery and, therefore, more gravitas—whether you're male or female, a leader or an emerging leader, in the corporate workplace or an entrepreneur.

CONCLUSION

When I was a little girl, about 10 years old, I found a stone axe in our garden.

This axe, as it was identified at the time by Aboriginal Affairs Queensland, was probably quarried in North Queensland and, having been found in South East Queensland, hinted at the fact that it was used for trading. It therefore became evidence for a much misunderstood—if not ignored—fact about Aboriginal trading between geographically diverse areas.

I discovered that it was one of only three other such axes ever found in the area. It was a real treasure, a true discovery. But I understood its importance, so I offered to return the axe to its original owners. However, this turned out to be harder than I thought it would be.

Speaking with those at the Queensland Environmental Protection Agency, they indicated that they had no place to display the axe. So it was suggested that I 'take the axe home and treasure it'. There was no one else that I could reach out to back then.

As it turned out, the time was not ripe for my axe. Today's advice is to replace such a find where it was found, with its presence reported to the First Peoples—State Relations, where there will be a record of it for posterity.

This experience reminded me, however, of the experience of voice innovator Alfred Wolfsohn, who did incredible work around the psychology of voice, but who remained 'forever frustrated that his work did not achieve wider acclaim and dissemination'[1] during his own lifetime. This was one of my reasons for writing this book—knowledge needs sharing—not for my own personal acclaim, but because of the importance of learning from lost knowledge that holds tremendous significance if we are to embrace better communication and gravitas.

The New Ways for Gravitas

In my research and through my own experiences, I have sensed a ripeness for new ways to address communication as well as renewed interest in gravitas in Western culture as a whole. This seems to be the antidote to the 'culturally induced autism'—or learned helplessness[2]—that we have been experiencing as a reflection of the culture of our more recent past. This culture (or 'zeitgeist') has been a thorn in our side, and doing nothing more than inhibiting two-way communication between speaker and audience.

The schools of communication since the 1960s have attempted to guide us. They have not. The appalling lack of confidence amongst women in particular, the lack of awareness of skills needed for communicating with gravitas by both sexes, such as body awareness, voice and gestures, as well as our loss of the ability to memorise, is breathtakingly severe. The modern rules (both taught and unspoken) instead seem to me to require speakers to remain static and still, posed behind a lectern with a microphone to amplify a voice they already feel self-conscious about. We are told to stop gesturing, not to smile too much, to remove emotion from the conversation and to speak with a serious (and deep!) tone, all of which is misinterpreted in our modern age as requirements for gravitas. What we are left with is someone with perhaps a key new medical invention, standing hidden on the stage, reading a poorly written speech with no clear message, and attempting to be motionless and lowering their voice for authority. They come off stage and, knowing they have read every word, think they have done a great professional job.

Let me make it clear. Everyone in the audience was bored, they retained no information, no emotion was raised and no influence was achieved. Quite simply, the listener may as well have had a nice cup of hot brew and read the key points in a more enthused way on their own in a coffee shop. Just as much actual connection and engagement would have been created.

Returning to Ancient Wisdom

In ancient Rome, the Emperor enters the city to a triumphal march. He rides in a horse-drawn carriage, raising him above the crowd, surrounded by warriors and onlookers waving flags. A cape flows from his back, caught by the movement of the wind, and he raises his hand high with his body wide open to the world. The claque encourages a wild chant—with the creaking of the carriage, the rattle of the stones underfoot and the screaming of praise, the noise is deafening.

In 2023, after his indictment in New Jersey, Donald Trump appears at an event to the loud deep voice of a man proclaiming the proposition, 'Ladies and gentlemen. The next President of the United States.' Trump moves swiftly to the exact centre of the doorway and stops. Behind him are several American flags draped artistically for the shot. The modern claque begins the chant in the audience of 'USA! USA! USA!' Trump opens his arms with his palms forward as a display of trust and follows this with a thumbs-up gesture as a sign of victory. He then paces the stage, from one side to the other, outstretching his arm, pointing to participants in the crowd to the far right and then far left, and making expressions as if to thank them for their support.

This kind of triumph has not been seen in the Western world since Hitler. It is highly influential. It is certainly embracing a new way of communicating, but at the moment it is most associated with seedy politicians and underhanded attempts at influence and, most importantly, with those that may not be using it for good.

Our challenge is two-fold. Firstly, if we are going to communicate better and with greater gravitas in our non-political daily lives, we need to grapple back these elements of audience participation for ourselves (to create that new model of two-way communication) and use them more widely in our communications for good. Secondly, we need to recognise the skills needed for two-way communication and gravitas in everything we see around us, and we need to become more aware of how we are being influenced by the communication prowess of others. If we perceive someone's intention as being good, then we can appreciate and even praise the communication (much like a modern version of claqueurs). If we see someone's intention as being inspired by personal gain or evil intent, then we need to identify that, protect ourselves from undue influence, despite the skill of the communicator, and be able to express our understanding of their true intentions to others.

Here, we are speaking of what the ancients called gravitas—the manner of trust and respect—and these skills are critical today to inspire others and bring about change and leadership in any field, whether you are a parent at a school meeting or leading an international organisation. Of course, you will not have a carriage and warriors, but you will have the awareness of the skills (canons) of rhetoric, understand the importance of nonverbal communication and be able to refocus on the missing aspect of delivery, all to build and create the confidence and trust you need to truly develop gravitas in the modern world.

In an orator, the acuteness of the logicians, the wisdom of the philosophers, the language almost of poetry, the memory of lawyers, the voice of tragedians, the gesture almost of the best actors, is required. Nothing therefore is more rarely found among mankind than a consummate orator. [3]

— Cicero

REFERENCES

Preface

1. Drucker, P (1969). *The Age of Discontinuity: Guidelines to our changing society*. Harper & Row. Peters, T & Waterman, R (1990). *In Search of Excellence*, Harper & Row Publishers. Freed, G (1992). *Fifth Generation Innovation. A. C. f. I. a. I. Competitiveness*. University of Sydney. Senge, P (1992). *The Fifth Discipline*. Random House. Handy, C (1994). The Empty Raincoat. Hutchinson.
2. Edelman Trust Barometer (2023). Global Report. Available at https://www.edelman.com.au/trust/2023/trust-barometer.

Introduction

1. CNBC Television (13 June 2023). Former President Donald Trump delivers remarks following his arraignment — 6/13/23. YouTube. Available at https://www.youtube.com/watch?v=QAvt4b0fGdQ.
2. McPherson, E, 9 News (5 November 2020). 'Trump wins almost 5 million more votes than at the 2016 election.' Available at https://www.9news.com.au/world/us-election-2020-trump-wins-almost-5-million-more-votes-than-in-2016/369e1d88-c3f1-44e7-b0aa-47875b39bfab.

3. Harris, R (2007). *Imperium: A Novel of Ancient Rome*. Gallery Books.
4. Fellows, A & Whitehead, E (Executive Producers). *Louis Theroux Interviews* (Series 1, Episode 4: 'Bear Grylls.' Available at https://iview.abc.net.au/video/ZW3572A004S00.
5. Swenson, A (2011). 'You make my heart beat faster: A quantitative study of the relationship between instructor immediacy, classroom community, and public speaking anxiety.' *UW-L Journal of Undergraduate Research XIV.* Available at https://www.uwlax.edu/globalassets/offices-services/urc/jur-online/pdf/2011/swenson.cst.pdf.

Chapter 1

1. Britannica. 'Greeks, Romans, and barbarians.' Available at https://www.britannica.com/topic/history-of-Europe/Greeks-Romans-and-barbarians.
2. Hooker, J (1976). *Mycenaean Greece*. Routledge.
3. 'Ancient History & Civilisation.' *Ancient Greece and Rome: An Encyclopedia for Students*. Available at https://erenow.net/ancient/ancient-greece-and-rome-an-encyclopedia-for-students-4-volume-set/316.php.
4. Shelton, J-A (1998). *As the Romans Did: A Sourcebook in Roman Social History*. Oxford University Press.
5. 'Ancient History & Civilisation.' *Ancient Greece and Rome: An Encyclopedia for Students*.
6. Wilson, D (2011). *The Rhetoric Companion: A Student's Guide to Power in Persuasion*. Canon Press.
7. Jebb, R (trans.) (1909). *The Rhetoric of Aristotle: A Translation*. Cambridge University Press.
8. Holland, G (2016). 'Delivery, Delivery, Delivery.' In: SE Porter and BR Dyer (eds), *Paul and Ancient Rhetoric: Accounting for Performance in the Rhetoric of Paul's Letters*. Cambridge University Press.
9. Jebb. *The Rhetoric of Aristotle: A Translation*.

10. Quintilian (2006). *Institutio Oratoria (Institutes of Oratory)*. L Honeycutt (ed); JS Watson (trans.). Available at https://kairos .technorhetoric.net/stasis/2017/honeycutt/quintilian/index.html (original work published 1856).
11. S Papaioannou, A Serafim & M Edwards (eds) (2021). *Brill's Companion to the Reception of Ancient Rhetoric*. Series: Brill's Companions to Classical Reception, Vol. 23. *Brill*.
12. Grant, A (2011). *Collected Works of Marcus Tullius Cicero*. BiblioLife.
13. Toogood, G (1995). *The Articulate Executive*. McGraw-Hill.
14. Saint Augustine (1953). *The Confessions; The City of God; On Christian Doctrine*. Blackwell.
15. Elias, J (2002). *History of Christian Education: Protestant, Catholic, and Orthodox Perspectives*. Krieger Pub Co.
16. Palmer, K (2020). *Diving into Rhetoric: A Rhetorical View of History, Communication, and Composition*. The Worry Free Writer.
17. Palmer. *Diving into Rhetoric*.
18. Elias. *History of Christian Education*.
19. Palmer. *Diving into Rhetoric*.
20. Wollacott, M (7 August 2023). 'What Is the Connection between Oratory and Rhetoric?' Available at https://www.language humanities.org/what-is-the-connection-between-oratory-and-rhetoric.htm.
21. Nguyen, TC (31 January 2021). 'The Early History of Communication.' ThoughtCo. Available at https://www.thoughtco .com/early-history-of-communication-4067897.
22. Wollacott. 'What Is the Connection between Oratory and Rhetoric?'
23. Cicero, MT; Caplan, C (trans.) (1954). *Rhetorica ad Herennium*. Harvard University Press.
24. P Bizzell & B Herzberg (eds) (2001). *The Rhetorical Tradition: Readings from Classical Times to the Present* (2nd edn). Bedford/ St. Martin's.
25. Quintilian. *Institutio Oratoria*.
26. Wilson. *The Rhetoric Companion*.
27. Quintilian. *Institutio Oratoria*.

28. Quintilian. *Institutio Oratoria.*
29. Hewlett, SA (2014). *Executive Presence: The Missing Link Between Merit and Success.* HarperCollins.
30. The University of Utah (2022). 'Writing and Rhetoric Studies.' Academic Advising Center: Undergraduate Studies. Available at https://advising.utah.edu/majors/quick-look/ writing-rhetoric-studies.php.
31. Rhetoric Society of Europe (2023). 'Rhetoric Programs in Europe (BA/MA).' Available at https://rhetoricsocietyeurope .eu/rhetoric-programs-in-europe/.
32. Wollacott. 'What Is the Connection between Oratory and Rhetoric?'
33. Quintilian. *Institutio Oratorio.*
34. Quintilian. *Institutio Oratoria.*
35. Cicero, MT; May, J & Wisse, J (trans.) (2001). *De Oratore (Cicero on the Ideal Orator).* Oxford University Press.
36. Quintilian. *Institutio Oratoria.*
37. Oxford English Dictionary (2023). Available at https://www .oed.com/dictionary/gravitas_n.
38. Merriam-Webster (2023). Available at https://www.merriam-webster.com/dictionary/gravitas.
39. Cambridge Dictionary (2023). Available at https://dictionary .cambridge.org/dictionary/english/gravitas.
40. Quintilian. *Institutio Oratoria.*
41. Quintilian. *Institutio Oratoria.*
42. Philo, L, Scaura, L & Brutus, I. *Restoring the Ancient Roman Virtues.* Available at https://romanrepublic.org/wip/virtues.pdf.
43. Australian National University. 'Rhetoric: The Art of Persuasion in the Ancient and Modern Worlds.' Available at https://programs andcourses.anu.edu.au/2021/course/clas3000#terms.
44. Newton, R (24 September 2020). 'Gravitas Is a Quality You Can Develop.' *Harvard Business Review.* Available at https://hbr .org/2020/09/gravitas-is-a-quality-you-can-develop.
45. Executive Presence Group. 'Research.' Available at https://www .executivepresencegroup.com/intelligence/research/.

Chapter 2

1. Quintilian. *Institutio Oratoria.*
2. Nazareno, M. 'Aristotle's Model of Communication.' Academia. Available at https://www.academia.edu/26760915/Aristotles_ Model_of_Communication.
3. Nazareno. 'Aristotle's Model of Communication.'
4. Jebb. *The Rhetoric of Aristotle: A Translation.*
5. Kincaid, D (1979). 'The Convergence Model of Communication. Honolulu: East-West Communication Institute.' Available at https://scholarspace.manoa.hawaii.edu/items/d5c61cc1-1e68-4cef-bb63-baf01dc0ac1c.
6. Aldrete, GS (2003). *Gestures and Acclamations in Ancient Rome (Ancient Society and History).* Johns Hopkins University Press.
7. Aldrete. *Gestures and Acclamations in Ancient Rome.*
8. Aldrete. *Gestures and Acclamations in Ancient Rome.*
9. History.com (12 June 2023). 'Augustus.' Available at https://www.history.com/topics/ancient-rome/emperor-augustus.
10. Shannon, CE (1948). 'A Mathematical Theory of Communication.' *Bell System Technical Journal.* Vol. 27, Issue 3. Available at doi:10.1002/j.1538-7305.1948.tb01338.x.
11. Communication Theory. 'Berlo's SMCR Model of Communication.' Available at https://www.communicationtheory.org/berlos-smcr-model-of-communication/.
12. Ackerman, CE (24 March 2018). 'Learned Helplessness: Seligman's Theory of Depression.' Positive Psychology. Available at https://positivepsychology.com/learned-helplessness-seligman-theory-depression-cure/.
13. Swan, K (2002). 'Building Learning Communities in Online Courses: The Importance of Interaction.' *Education, Communication & Information*, Vol. 2, Issue 1. Available at http://dx.doi.org/10.1080/1463631022000005016.
14. Crocq, M-A (2015). 'A History of Anxiety: From Hippocrates to DSM.' *Dialogues in Clinical Neuroscience.* Vol. 17, Issue 3. Available at https://www.ncbi.nlm.nih.gov/pmc/articles/PMC4610616/.

15. Crocq. 'A History of Anxiety: From Hippocrates to DSM.'
16. Crocq. 'A History of Anxiety: From Hippocrates to DSM.'
17. Marks, H (13 November 2021). 'Stage Fright (Performance Anxiety).' Anxiety & Panic Disorders Guide. WebMD. Available at https://www.webmd.com/anxiety-panic/stage-fright-performance-anxiety.
18. Goleman, D (1995). *Emotional Intelligence: Why It Can Matter More Than IQ*. Bloomsbury.
19. Goleman. *Emotional Intelligence*.
20. Koller, WN (2017). *Subclinical Depression, Anxiety, and Alexithymia: Implications for Implicit and Explicit Emotion Regulation*. Honors Theses. Bates College. Available at https://scarab.bates.edu/cgi/viewcontent.cgi?article=1246&context=honorstheses.
21. Goleman. *Emotional Intelligence*.
22. Cooperrider, K (4 May 2020). 'Smell you later.' Kensy Cooperrider blog. Available at http://kensycooperrider.com/blog/smell-you-later.
23. Stanton, M (11 January 2021). 'Greeting customs from around the world (and how to do them properly).' Lonely Planet. Available at https://www.lonelyplanet.com/articles/greeting-customs-around-the-world.

Chapter 3

1. Aldrete. *Gestures and Acclamations of Ancient Rome*.
2. Quintilian. *Institutio Oratoria*.
3. Quintilian. *Institutio Oratoria*.
4. Quintilian. *Institutio Oratoria*.
5. Quintilian. *Institutio Oratoria*.
6. Quintilian. *Institutio Oratoria*.
7. Quintilian. *Institutio Oratoria*.
8. Quintilian. *Institutio Oratoria*.
9. Quintilian. *Institutio Oratoria*.
10. Quintilian. *Institutio Oratoria*.

11. Quintilian. *Institutio Oratoria.*

12. Müller-Preis, E (1989). Personal Correspondence: Body, Movement and Voice. London.

13. Birdwhistell, RL (2021). *Introduction to Kinesics: An Annotation System for Analysis of Body Motion and Gesture.* Hassell Street Press.

14. Pease, A & Pease, B (24 September 2006). 'The Definitive Book of Body Language.' *New York Times.* https://www.nytimes.com/2006/09/24/books/chapters/0924-1st-peas.html.

15. Mehrabian, A (1972). *Nonverbal Communication.* Routledge.

16. Ekman, P & Friesen, WV (1969). 'The Repertoire or Nonverbal Behavior: Categories, Origins, Usage, and Coding.' *Semiotica.* Available at https://doi.org/10.1515/semi.1969.1.1.49.

17. Lessac, A (1997). *Body Wisdom: The Use and Training of the Human Body.* Drama Book Specialists.

18. Raphael, BN (1997). 'A Consumer's Guide to Voice and Speech Training.' In: M Hampton & B Acker (eds), *The Vocal Vision.* Applause.

19. Lessac. *Body Wisdom.*

20. Barlow, W (2001). *The Alexander Principle: How to Use Your Body Without Stress.* Orion Publishing.

21. Kretschmer, E (1925). *Physique and Character: An Investigation of the Nature of Constitution and of the Theory.* Routledge.

22. Sheldon, WH (1940). *The Varieties of Human Physique. An Introduction to Constitutional Psychology.* Harper & Brothers.

23. Efron, D (1941). *Gesture and Environment.* King's Crown Press.

24. Pease, A & Pease, B (2017). *The Definitive Book Of Body Language.* HQ Non Fiction.

25. Navarro, J & Karlins, M (2008). *What Every Body Is Saying: An Ex-FBI Agent's Guide to Speed-Reading People.* HarperCollins.

26. Wezowski, K & Wezowski, P (2018). *Without Saying a Word: Master the Science of Body Language and Maximize Your Success.* AMACOM.

27. Sullivan, H (1954). *The Psychiatric Interview.* Norton.

28. Whipple, R (2018). 'Body Language 6 Folding Arms.' The Trust Ambassador. Available at https://thetrustambassador .com/2018/12/15/body-language-6-folding-arms.
29. Cherry, N (1996). 'Developing Reflective Practice.' Royal Melbourne Institute of Technology University. Available at https://researchrepository.rmit.edu.au/esploro/outputs/doctoral/ Developing-reflective-practice/9921861357001341.
30. Barbiero, D (20 June 2005). *Dictionary of Philosophy of Mind.* Philosophy of *Mind.* Available at http://philosophy.uwaterloo .ca/MindDict.
31. Cairnes, M (1998). *Approaching the Corporate Heart.* Simon & Schuster.
32. Cairnes. *Approaching the Corporate Heart.*
33. Polanyi, M (1969). *Knowing and Being.* University of Chicago Press.
34. Nonaka, I (2007). 'The knowledge-creating company.' *Harvard Business Review.* Available at https://hbr.org/2007/07/the-knowledge-creating-company.
35. Lamorisse, A (1956). *The Red Balloon.* Films Montsouris.

Chapter 4

1. Quintilian. *Institutio Oratoria.*
2. Quintilian. *Institutio Oratoria.*
3. Wardle, D (2000). *Valerius Maximus: Memorable Deeds and Sayings.* Clarendon Ancient History Series. Acta Classica.
4. Loeb Classical Library. *Fragmentary Republican Latin: Oratory.* Harvard University Press. Available at https://www.loebclassics .com/view/fragmentary_republican_latin-oratory/2019/pb_ LCL541.161.xml.
5. Quintilian. *Institutio Oratoria.*
6. Aldrete. *Gestures and Acclamations in Ancient Rome.*
7. Quintilian. *Institutio Oratoria.*
8. Drumann, W (1906). *Geschichte Roms in Seinem Übergange von der Republikanischen zur Monarchischen Verfassung, oder Pompeius,*

Caesar, Cicero und Ihre Zeitgenossen (in German). Vol. 3 (2nd edn). Gebrüder Borntraeger.

9. Britannica. 'Pompey the Great: Roman statesman.' Available at https://www.britannica.com/biography/Pompey-the-Great.

10. Aldrete. *Gestures and Acclamations in Ancient Rome.*

11. Aldrete. *Gestures and Acclamations in Ancient Rome.*

12. Summers, J & Smith, B (2014). *The Communication Skills Handbook.* Wiley.

13. O'Toole, G (2020). *Communication: Core Interpersonal Skills for Healthcare Professionals.* Elsevier.

14. Kuhnke, E (2012). *Communication Skills For Dummies.* Wiley.

15. Wilson. *The Rhetoric Companion.*

16. Birdwhistell. *Introduction to Kinesics.*

17. Wolf, J (2 June 2020). 'The importance of nonverbal communication in virtual meetings.' SmartBrief. Available at https://corp.smartbrief.com/original/2020/06/importance-nonverbal-communication-virtual-meetings.

18. Fouts, M (30 September 2021). 'Body Language In A Virtual World: How To Communicate Your Message Effectively.' *Forbes.* Available at https://www.forbes.com/sites/forbescoachescouncil/2021/09/30/body-language-in-a-virtual-world-how-to-communicate-your-message-effectively/?sh=33d6ae764964.

19. Mader, G (2000). 'Blocked Eyes and Ears: The Eloquent Gestures at Augustine, Conf., VI, 8, 13.' In: *L'antiquité Classique.*

20. Amalar of Metz; Knibbs, E (trans.) (2014). *On the Liturgy, Volume 1, Books 1–2.* Harvard University Press.

21. Falque, E (2011). Gesture and Speech: Hugh of Saint-Victor's De Institutione novitiorum. *Revue des Sciences Philosophiques et Théologiques.* Vol. 95, Issue 2, pp. 383–412.

22. Gale Ambassadors (12 April 2018). 'Nazi Germany, Ancient Rome: The appropriation of classical culture for the formulation of national identity.' The Gale Review. Available at https://review.gale.com/2018/04/12/nazi-germany-ancient-rome-the-appropriation-of-classical-culture-for-the-formulation-of-national-identity/.

23. Pick, D (2012). *The Pursuit of the Nazi Mind: Hitler, Hess, and the Analysts*. Oxford University Press.

24. Quintilian. *Institutio Oratoria*.

25. The Gladiator Guide (13 September 2022). 'Gladiator: Nazis, History & Roman gestures.' YouTube. Available at https://www.youtube.com/watch?v=U63pnq0ihOw.

26. de Jorio, A; Kendon, A (trans.) (2000). *Gesture in Naples and Gesture in Classical Antiquity*. Indiana University Press.

27. Testimonial. Andrew Mackenzie, ex-CEO BHP; Chair: Shell.

28. Hall, J (2004). 'Cicero and Quintilian on the Oratorical Use of Hand Gestures.' *The Classical Quarterly*. Vol. 54, Issue 1, pp. 143–160. Cambridge University Press.

29. Quintilian. *Institutio Oratoria*.

30. Quintilian. *Institutio Oratoria*.

31. Quintilian. *Institutio Oratoria*.

32. Quintilian. *Institutio Oratoria*.

33. Quintilian. *Institutio Oratoria*.

34. Ellsberg, M (2010). *The Power of Eye Contact: Your Secret for Success in Business, Love, and Life*. William Morrow Paperbacks.

35. Brych, M, Murali, S & Händel, B (2021). 'How the motor aspect of speaking influences the blink rate.' *PLoS One*. Vol. 16, Issue 10, e025832. Available at https://www.ncbi.nlm.nih.gov/pmc/articles/PMC8500445/.

Chapter 5

1. Quintilian. *Institutio Oratoria*.

2. Toogood. *The Articulate Executive*.

3. von Leden, H (1982). A Cultural History of the Human Voice: 1982 Paul Moore Lecture. In: Sataloff, RT. *Voice Perspectives*. Singular Publishing Group Inc.

4. Moses, PJ (1954). *The Voice of Neurosis*. Grune & Stratton.

5. Abram, D (1996). *The Spell of the Sensuous: Perception and Language in a More-than-human World*. Pantheon Books.

6. von Leden. A Cultural History of the Human Voice.

7. von Leden. A Cultural History of the Human Voice.

8. von Leden. A Cultural History of the Human Voice.

9. Aldrete. *Gestures and Acclamations in Ancient Rome.*

10. Aldrete. *Gestures and Acclamations in Ancient Rome.*

11. Quintilian. *Institutio Oratoria.*

12. Quintilian. *Institutio Oratoria.*

13. Quintilian. *Institutio Oratoria.*

14. Quintilian. *Institutio Oratoria.*

15. Quintilian. *Institutio Oratoria.*

16. Quintilian. *Institutio Oratoria.*

17. Quintilian. *Institutio Oratoria.*

18. Quintilian. *Institutio Oratoria.*

19. Quintilian. *Institutio Oratoria.*

20. Quintilian. *Institutio Oratoria.*

21. Quintilian. *Institutio Oratoria.*

22. Birdwhistell, RL (1970). *Kinesics and context: Essays on Body Motion Communication.* Ballantine. Philpott, JS (1983). *The relative contribution to meaning of verbal and nonverbal channels of communication: A meta-analysis.* Master's thesis: University of Nebraska.

23. Mehrabian. *Nonverbal Communication.*

24. Yaffe, P (October 2011). 'The 7% Rule: Fact, Fiction, or Misunderstanding.' Ubiquity. Available at https://ubiquity.acm.org/article.cfm?id=2043156.

25. Leathers, DG (1997). *Successful Nonverbal Communication: Principles and Applications.* Pearson.

26. Mohan, T (1997). *Communicating: Theory and Practice.* Nelson Thomson Learning.

27. Toogood. *The Articulate Executive.*

28. Zuckerman, M, Hodgins, H & Miyake, K (1990). 'The Vocal Attractiveness Stereotype: Replication and Elaboration.' *Journal of Nonverbal Behavior.* Vol. 14, pp. 97–112. Available at https://doi.org/10.1007/BF01670437.

29. Berry, D (2000). 'Attractiveness, Attraction, and Sexual Selection: Evolutionary Perspectives on the Form and Function of Physical Attractiveness.' *Advances in Experimental Social Psychology.* Vol. 32, pp. 273–342. Available at https://doi .org/10.1016/S0065-2601(00)80007-6.

30. Street, RL & Hopper, R (1982). 'A Model of Speech Style Evaluation.' In: EB Ryan & H Giles (eds), *Attitudes towards Language Variations: Social and Applied Contexts.* Edward Arnold.

31. Street & Hopper. 'A Model of Speech Style Evaluation.'

32. Scherer, K, London, H & Wolf, J (1973). 'The Voice of Confidence: Paralinguistic Cues and Audience Evaluation.' *Journal of Research in Personality.* Vol. 7, Issue 1, pp. 31–44. Available at https://doi.org/10.1016/0092-6566(73)90030-5.

33. Jurich, A & Jurich, J (1974). 'The Effect of Cognitive Moral Development upon the Selection of Premarital Sexual Standards.' *Journal of Marriage and the Family.* Vol. 36, Issue 4, pp. 736–741. Available at https://doi.org/10.2307/350356.

34. Hosman, L (1989). 'The Evaluative Consequences of Hedges, Hesitations, and Intensifies Powerful and Powerless Speech Styles.' *Human Communication Research.* Vol. 15, Issue 3, pp. 383–406. Available at https://onlinelibrary.wiley.com/doi/abs/10 .1111/j.1468-2958.1989.tb00190.x.

35. Kramer, E (1963). 'Judgment of Personal Characteristics and Emotions from Nonverbal Properties of Speech.' *Psychological Bulletin.* Vol. 60, Issue 4, pp. 408–420. Available at https:// psycnet.apa.org/doiLanding?doi=10.1037%2Fh0044890.

36. Pearce, W & Conklin, F (1971). 'Nonverbal vocalic communi- cation and perceptions of a speaker.' *Speech Monographs.* Vol. 38, Issue 3, pp. 235–241. Available at https://doi.org/10.1080/ 03637757109375715.

37. Pearce & Conklin. 'Nonverbal vocalic communication and perceptions of a speaker.'

38. Griffiths, R (1990). 'Speech Rate and NNS Comprehension: A Preliminary Study in Time-Benefit Analysis.' *Language Learning.* Vol. 40, Issue 3, pp. 311–336.

39. Dean, J (2022). 'Talking fast may be a sign of intelligence and has other advantages.' PsyBlog. Available at https://www.spring.org.uk/2022/11/talking-fast.php.

40. Frip, P (13 June 2023). Facebook post providing expert advice when you are speaking too quickly. Available at https://www.facebook.com/photo/?fbid=726290292829547&set=a.419401016851811.

41. Frip Facebook post providing expert advice when you are speaking too quickly.

42. Frip. Facebook post providing expert advice when you are speaking too quickly.

43. Mahler, L (2015). *Resonate: For People Who Need to Be Heard.* Penguin Random House.

Chapter 6

1. Institute of Leadership & Management (2011). 'Ambition and Gender at Work.' Available at https://www.institutelm.com/static/uploaded/6151ed78-0ad1-495d-960e0ae40413b572.pdf.

2. Glassdoor Economic Research (9 March 2022). '85% of employed women believe they deserve a pay raise; more salary transparency can help.' Available at https://www.glassdoor.com/research/pay-transparency-survey-2022/.

3. Babcock, L and Laschever, S (2021). *Women Don't Ask: Negotiation and the Gender Divide.* Princeton University Press.

4. Shipman, C & Kay, K (2014). *The Confidence Code.* HarperCollins.

5. Reilly, D, Neumann, D & Andrews, G (2022). 'Gender Differences in Self-Estimated Intelligence: Exploring the Male Hubris, Female Humility Problem.' *Frontiers in Psychology.* Vol. 13. Available at https://www.ncbi.nlm.nih.gov/pmc/articles/PMC8858829/.

6. Karpowitz, C, Mendelberg, T & Shaker, L (August 2012). 'Gender Inequality in Deliberative Participation.' *American Political Science Review.* Available at https://www.bu.edu/wgs/files/2014/12/Karpowitz-et-al.-2012.pdf.

7. Hewlett. *Executive Presence.*
8. Quintilian. *Institutio Oratoria.*
9. Rennung, M Blum, J, and Göritz, A (2016). 'To Strike a Pose: No Stereotype Backlash for Power Posing Women.' *Frontiers in Psychology.* Vol. 7. Available at https://www.ncbi.nlm.nih.gov/pmc/articles/PMC5037219/.
10. Rennung, Blum & Göritz. 'To Strike a Pose: No Stereotype Backlash for Power Posing Women.'
11. Whipple, R (2020). 'Body Language 90 Blinking Rate.' The Trust Ambassador. Available at https://thetrustambassador .com/2020/08/13/body-language-90-blinking-rate/.
12. Re, D, O'Connor, J, Bennett, P & Feinberg, D (2012). 'Preferences for Very Low and Very High Voice Pitch in Humans.' *PLoS One.* Vol. 7, Issue 3, e32719. Available at https://www.ncbi.nlm.nih.gov/pmc/articles/PMC3293852/.
13. Kim, M (6 July 2022). 'Think Leader, Think Deep Voice? CEO Voice Pitch and Gender.' *Academy of Management.* Available at https://journals.aom.org/doi/abs/10.5465/AMBPP .2022.17778abstract.
14. Kim. 'Think Leader, Think Deep Voice?'
15. Quintilian. *Institutio Oratoria.*
16. Hesketh, R (27 July 2020). 'U.K. Companies With More Women on Executive Boards Outperform on Profits.' Bloomberg. Available at https://www.bloomberg.com/news/articles/2020-07-27/u-k-firms-with-more-women-on-exec-boards-outperform-on-profits.
17. Workplace Gender Equality Agency. 'Women in Leadership.' Available at https://www.wgea.gov.au/women-in-leadership.

Chapter 7

1. Quintilian. *Institutio Oratoria.*
2. Quintilian. *Institutio Oratoria.*
3. Cicero, MT; Caplan, C (trans.). *Rhetorica ad Herennium.*

4. Quintilian. *Institutio Oratoria*.

5. Dayan, A (July/August 2019). 'Omne Trium Perfectum: Three may really be the charm.' Modern Aesthetics. Available at https://modernaesthetics.com/articles/2019-july-aug/omne-trium-perfectum.

6. Brown University (18 May 2004). 'Scents will not rouse us from slumber, says new Brown University study.' Science Daily. Available at https://www.sciencedaily.com/releases/2004/05/040518075747.htm.

7. Quintilian. *Institutio Oratoria*.

8. Wilson. *The Rhetoric Companion*.

9. McCabe, J (2015). 'Location, Location, Location! Demonstrating the Mnemonic Benefit of the Method of Loci.' *Teaching of Psychology*. Vol. 42, Issue 2. Available at https://doi.org/10.1177/0098628315573143.

10. Legge, E, Madan, C, Ng, E & Caplan J (2012). 'Building a Memory Palace in Minutes: Equivalent Memory Performance Using Virtual versus Conventional Environments with the Method of Loci.' *Acta Psychologica*. Vol. 141, Issue 3, pp. 380–390. Available at https://linkinghub.elsevier.com/retrieve/pii/S000169181200145X.

11. Robinson, T (ed) (1979). *Contrasting Arguments: An Edition of the Dissoi Logoi*. Arno Press.

12. Cicero, MT; Caplan, C (trans.). *Rhetorica ad Herennium*.

13. Gwynn, A (1926). *Roman Education from Cicero to Quintilian*. Clarendon Press.

14. Quintilian. *Institutio Oratoria*.

15. Cicero, MT; May, J & Wisse, J (trans.). *De Oratore (Cicero on the Ideal Orator)*.

16. Cicero, MT; May, J & Wisse, J (trans.). *De Oratore (Cicero on the Ideal Orator)*.

17. Aldrete. *Gestures and Acclamations of Ancient Rome*.

18. Duarte, N (2008). *Slide:ology: The Art and Science of Creating Great Presentations*. O'Reilly Media.

Conclusion

1. Newham, P (1992). 'Jung and Alfred Wolfsohn: Analytical Psychology and the Singing Voice.' *Journal of Analytical Psychology*. Vol. 37, Issue 3, pp. 323–336.
2. Hiley, T (2003). *Living and Working in the First Person: Emancipating the 'Silent' Voice and the 'Deaf' Ear*. Doctoral dissertation, RMIT University.
3. Cicero, MT; May, J & Wisse, J (trans.). *De Oratore (Cicero on the Ideal Orator)*.